"No Matter How Thin You Slice It, It's Still Baloney"

A Collection of Outrageous Quotes

Edited by Jean Arbeiter

Illustrations by Jeff Danziger

QUILL *New York* *1984*

FOR *Kenneth Schwartz*

BOOKS BY JEAN ARBEITER

Pegs to Hang Ideas On with Marjorie P. Katz (M. Evans, 1973)

Womanlist with Marjorie P. K. Weiser (Atheneum, 1981)

Permanent Addresses with Linda D. Cirino (M. Evans, 1983)

Library of Congress Cataloging in Publication Data

Main entry under title:

"No matter how thin you slice it, it's still baloney."

1. Quotations, English. I. Arbeiter, Jean S.
II. Title: No matter how thin you slice it, it's still baloney.
[PN6083.B7 1984b]   081   83-13687
ISBN 0-688-01368-6 (pbk.)

Printed in the United States of America

First Quill Edition

1 2 3 4 5 6 7 8 9 10

PREFACE

Baloney is as old as man's tendency to aggrandize himself or to cover his nether regions. Nero, for example, once remarked, "I am not a wretched musician. I am a very great one," a comment that soon proved to be gratuitous.

Today, Baloney has grown to epic proportions. It is everywhere—in the marketplace and the newspapers, on the TV screen and, on some occasions, even in the White House and the Congress. The purpose of this book is to amuse, and perhaps illuminate, via the plentiful commodity of Baloney. Baloney is fun because it's so inventive that it can't be boring. Rarely an outright fabrication, it usually stems from wishful thinking, self-adulation, pomposity, an oversupply of piety, or pure miscalculation.

The isolation from everyday life experienced by some rich people and celebrities has led to remarks that seem perfectly reasonable to their authors but screamingly funny to the hoi polloi who encounter them. J. Paul Getty's earnest explanation—"It's rude and inconsiderate to overtip. It only makes things difficult—and embarrassing for people who are not as rich as I am"—is an outstanding example. "The very rich are not like you and me," F. Scott Fitzgerald wrote, and clearly their Baloney is different too.

A charming category of Baloney consists of mix-ups, malapropisms, and simplicities that have no dark side but are just engaging. Casey Stengelisms belong to this group, along with many remarks of Chicago's former mayor, Richard Daley: "I resent the insinuendos," "The policeman isn't there to create disorder; the policeman is there to *preserve* disorder." This kind of Baloney is appealing because all of us have tongues and know how easily they can become knotted.

A common variety of Baloney consists of statements that were made with perfectly good intentions but have been proved incorrect by the passage of time. Included in this category are allegations that the sun moves around the earth, that the *Titanic* is unsinkable, that rocket ships will never get off the ground, and that the Edsel is bound to sell.

The true glory of Baloney lies in its many guises, its flexibility, its ability to amaze, and its capacity to multiply. It lives. It flows. The definitive words on this subject, however, have been uttered by heads much wiser than mine. Here they are in a couple of nutshells:

"No matter how thin you slice it, it's still baloney."
—ALFRED E. SMITH, 1936

"Self-justification is worse than the original offense."
—Middle Eastern proverb

"Hypocrisy is the homage vice pays to virtue."
—LA ROCHEFOUCAULD

"It's a great art to know how to sell wind."
—CONFUCIUS

"Ninety-nine percent of everything is bullshit."
—THEODORE STURGEON

"It's the same old shit. Only the flies are different."
—Old Portuguese saying

CONTENTS

CONTENTS

CELEBRITIES

"I don't know anything about music. In my line I don't have to."
　　　—ELVIS PRESLEY, 1957

"Nobody's going to bother me. After all, I took care of myself all my life."
　　　—JIMMY HOFFA

"I'm the most liberated woman in the world. Any woman can be liberated if she wants to be. First, she has to convince her husband."
　　　—MARTHA MITCHELL

"Smoking kills. If you're killed, you've lost a very important part of your life."
　　　—BROOKE SHIELDS, on her desire to be a spokesperson for a governmental antismoking campaign, 1981

"When women throw themselves at you all the time, sometimes the only way to treat them is badly."
　　　—JACK NICHOLSON, 1976

"I hate violence. If some security geezer hurts a kid, I'll bust him."
>—ALEX HARVEY, British rock star

"I sometimes feel bad about how much I make as a teenager but we do get ripped off by the government. Jeez, someday I've got to do something about that."
>—LINDA BLAIR, star of *The Exorcist*, 1977

"I am criticized for getting jobs because of my name, but I only use it when I have to."
>—SUSAN FORD, 1978; as photographer and presidential daughter, she earned $100,000 in one year

"Vietnamese kids are toilet trained by the time they can sit, and they don't seem to have problems."
>—JANE FONDA, engaging in cross-cultural comparisons

"I would never use the holy sacrament of marriage for publicity reasons."
>—TINY TIM, of his marriage to Vicki Budinger on Johnny Carson's *Tonight Show,* December 17, 1969

"This marriage is going to last a long, long time."
>—DEBBIE REYNOLDS, before her June 17, 1954, marriage to singer Eddie Fisher. They divorced in 1959.

"When Nick Hilton and I floated down the aisle, I thought it was for keeps."
>—ELIZABETH TAYLOR

"Don't worry, Eddie. It will pass. Richard must always have these flings with leading ladies."
>—EDDIE FISHER, recalling Sybil Burton's statement to him on the set of *Cleopatra* (1963)

"He left me."
>—ELIZABETH TAYLOR, filing for divorce from Eddie Fisher, 1964

"I shall never leave Sybil. She loves and understands me, and thinks I'm a genius."
>—RICHARD BURTON, to Hollywood columnist Sheilah Graham

"Ten years of marriage has brought me a stability I have never known before."
>—ELIZABETH TAYLOR, 1972

"I genuinely do not believe in divorce."
—ELIZABETH TAYLOR, 1965

"We will never be separated."
—ELIZABETH TAYLOR, 1968

"It's one of our greatest inventions. Monogamy allows a man to enjoy his woman and family with a reasonable amount of safety and comfort. Polygamy requires him to lie and deceive. With Elizabeth, I don't have to lie, and there's nothing to cheat about."
—RICHARD BURTON, 1968

"I'm ugly."
—ELIZABETH TAYLOR to Polly Bergen

"I will retire before I'm forty."
—ELIZABETH TAYLOR

"The good thing about my life is that one week I'm single and the next I'm not."
—DIANE VON FÜRSTENBERG

"I didn't even know the man. But I'm sure he was very nice."
—PATTY DUKE ASTIN, of her thirteen-day marriage to rock promoter Michael Tell

"Our marriage was into the clinging stage. Now we are into distancing. We're going to rotate the house and we even rotate the cars. We've been separated for four months, and it's a growing experience."
—TALIA SHIRE, on her separation from David Shire, 1978

"We're trying to work out the spatial conditions of our relationship. We need our own space right now."

  —STAN DRAGOTI, advertising man, on his split with Cheryl
   Tiegs, 1979

"We drew up a formula for a happy marriage and we're following it. Bet on us."

  —JANET LEIGH, to Sidney Skolsky, of her marriage to Tony
   Curtis, May 3, 1953

"There's an awful lot of cynicism everywhere about marriage, so much that's negative. Well, we like to think we make being married a positive thing. There's this myth in America about romance ending the minute marriage begins. I think we're showing people something different. We're married, we're in love, we kid each other a lot, but we're still in love."

  —CHER, when married to Sonny

"We are separating not to destroy but to save our marriage."

  —BARBRA STREISAND and ELLIOTT GOULD, February 13,
   1969

"We're no longer trying to save our marriage. What we've saved is a nice working relationship which we didn't have before."

  —ELLIOTT GOULD, November 1970

"He adores Ann, but he wanted the divorce because the marriage didn't work. It's a paradox."

  —MARVIN MITCHELSON, Richard Harris's attorney for his
   divorce from Ann Turkel, 1981

"I think a man can have two, maybe three love affairs while he is married. But three is the absolute maximum. After that you are cheating."

  —YVES MONTAND, 1982

"Maybe we live a superficial life but in seven days I see more people than anyone. At least, I'll know who to intensify with."

>   —DIANE VON FÜRSTENBERG, of her life with Prince Egon von Fürstenberg, 1973

"I want a cause."

>   —DIANE VON FÜRSTENBERG, at La Cirque restaurant, 1981

"She feels it's part of her early life that doesn't have anything to do with her life today."

>   —Stephen Morello, spokesman for EVANGELINE GOULETAS-CAREY, explaining why she had not mentioned that she had been married three times rather than two times before her 1981 wedding to Hugh Carey

"And I tell you that if Saint Paul were alive today, he would go to Paolo Grassi [head of the Italian Broadcasting Corporation] and ask him for more program time on TV."

>   —POPE JOHN PAUL II, quoted in "Pope Likes TV Medium," *Variety*, September 13, 1978

"Believe me, I have a high respect for the bulldogged way in which our president has been able to continue to administrate this government, in spite of the articulate liberal press—whose only purpose is to sell toilet paper and Toyotas—and in spite of the ambitious politicians."

>   —JOHN WAYNE, of the Nixon administration

"I feel that the people who were voted into office must have the intelligence to know what to do and that everybody should have faith in them."

>   —PAMELA ANNE ELDRED, Miss America 1970, on the role of the electorate

"Who knows who should be president and if anybody should have a big interest in determining those things. Shouldn't Standard Oil? I mean, they have more to gain and more to lose. If something terrible happens to Standard Oil a lot of people will be out of jobs. . . . We need them . . . we need their services, we need jobs from them, and they are in a better position to decide what's going to be good for the economic climate of the country and the rest of the world."
　　　　—LINDA RONSTADT, on the role of the electorate, 1978

"You'll never be anything. You'll never get anywhere singing in that sissy voice."
　　　　—The parents of Tiny Tim

"I can tell you flatly, he can't last."
　　　　—JACKIE GLEASON, on Elvis Presley, 1956

"They [the Beatles] are a passing phase. All are symptoms of the uncertainty of the times and the confusion about us."
　　　　—BILLY GRAHAM, 1963

"In the excitatory state that the Beatles place these youngsters into, these young people will do anything they are told to do. . . . One day, when the revolution is ripe, the Communists could put the Beatles on TV and could mass hypnotize American youth. This scares the wits out of me."
　　　　—THE REVEREND DAVID NOEBEL, 1965

"I work only according to God's directions."
　　　　—IDI AMIN, 1974

"God sent me to America in the role of a doctor."
　　　　—THE REVEREND SUN MYUNG MOON, 1977

"I think God is groovy. He had a great publicity agent."
>   —P. J. PROBY, rock star

"If God came into my room, I'd obviously be awed, but I don't think I'd feel humble. I might cry, but I know he'd dig me like mad."
>   —MARC BOLAN, rock star of T Rex, killed in a car crash in 1977

"Pop is the perfect religious vehicle. It's as if God had come down to earth and seen all the ugliness that was being created and chosen pop to be the great force for love and beauty."
>   —DONOVAN, 1968

"Elton doesn't waste money. . . . He *likes* cars."
>   —ELTON JOHN's manager, on why his client bought a Rolls-Royce and sold it three weeks later for another in a different color

"I love money. The origin of this joy of money is my Spanish mysticism. In the Middle Ages the alchemists wanted everything they touched to turn to gold. This is the best kind of spiritualization."
>   —Salvador Dalí, in a *Playboy* interview, July 1964

"If God didn't want me to have these things, I wouldn't have them."
>   —ELVIS PRESLEY, to his girl friend, Linda Thompson, on his prosperity

"I never met him but I expect to see him in heaven. He was deeply religious, especially during the last two years of his life."
>   —BILLY GRAHAM, on Elvis Presley

"[Reagan] is the best president we've had this century. Let's give the man a chance."
>   —JOHN W. HINCKLEY

"You are suggesting I have some sort of romantic attachment. I have no relationship with her, just a passing acquaintance for two nights."

> —MICK JAGGER, on Margaret Trudeau

"Scooter was one of my best, closest, dearest friends, and he still is."

> —GREG ALLMAN, 1976, after he testified against his good friend and road manager, Scooter Herring, in a drug trial. Allman received immunity in return for his testimony; Herring, who had once saved Allman's life after an overdose, got a seventy-five-year sentence for supplying the rock star with a half gram of cocaine daily.

"We probably were everything that a man and woman should be to each other. He was my best friend."

> —CLAUDINE LONGET, 1977, on trial for "reckless manslaughter" of her lover, Vladimir "Spider" Sabich, world pro skiing champ

"A good writer is one who produces books that people read. . . . So if I'm selling millions, I'm good."

> —JACQUELINE SUSANN

"I really had to act, 'cause I didn't have any lines."

> —MARILYN CHAMBERS, on her performance in the porn movie *Behind the Green Door*

"I went from a 36 bust to a 34 bust. The suit was too big. I couldn't go on stage and represent New York State like that."

> —DEBORAH ANN FOUNTAIN, Miss New York State 1981, disqualified from the Miss U.S.A. pageant for putting padding in her swimsuit. Her explanation was that she had lost weight.

"I realize about myself that I am, for all my passions, implacably, I think almost *unfailingly* fair; objective, *just.*"
    —WILLIAM F. BUCKLEY, JR., in *Cruising Speed* (1971)

"It's not fatness. It is development."
        —ANITA EKBERG, on why she had no need to take up dieting, 1974

"There's 150 million times more beer drinkers than there is Presidents."
        —BILLY CARTER, in answer to charges that he was shaming his brother, 1978

"I'm a liar, but an honest one."
        —FEDERICO FELLINI, film director, 1974

"The truth is, we didn't promote ourselves any more than the other nominees. People that came to see my stage show were already in town for another event—we didn't fly them in. And the luncheon at our home wasn't anything. We only served cold cuts."

—PIA ZADORA, 1982, answering charges that she and her multimillionaire husband, Meshulam Riklis, used influence to win her the Hollywood Foreign Press Association "New Star of the Year" Golden Globe Award. Members of the association were wined and dined at the couple's Beverly Hills mansion.

"I don't know anything about the externalism of being in the kitchen but I certainly know about ennui."

—LOUISE LASSER, on housewifery

"If I'd played ball with the producers in Hollywood I could have made it long ago as an actress. But I couldn't. Someone like Grace Kelly came along looking every inch a lady, and they'd give her a chance to act. Producers wouldn't attack her. But me! As soon as I walked in they started chasing me around the desks."

—LINDA CHRISTIAN, 1962

"Everyone should rise up and say, 'Thank you, Mr. President, for bombing Haiphong.'"

—MARTHA MITCHELL, at the Midwest Republican Women's Conference, 1972

"I am the only man in the world who can go and be loved by the Jews as much as the Moslems."

—MUHAMMAD ALI, in a radio interview, explaining why President Carter should make him an ambassador for world peace

"What Dom Perignon is to champagne, I am to acting."
>—TRUMAN CAPOTE, before starting work on his role in *Murder by Death* (1976)

"You know, *we don't fuck around,* worrying about eleven people dying. . . ."
>—PETER TOWNSHEND, of The Who, on the eleven fans who were crushed to death outside Cincinnati's Riverfront Coliseum just before a Who concert, December 3, 1980

"We don't really enjoy these things, you know."
>—RALPH STEADMAN, graphic satirist for *Rolling Stone,* of an incident in which he and reporter Hunter S. Thompson sprayed a waiter with chemical Mace, 1974. The pair, who were involved in many similar escapades, claimed, "We're not destructive—we're outraged, shocked and frustrated. There's no malevolence involved."

"I think if I weren't so beautiful, maybe I'd have more character."
>—JERRY HALL, model who took Mick Jagger away from Bianca, 1978

"Do the Stones use drugs? No, never."
>—MICK JAGGER

"I'm not a coke user, and I hadn't used that stuff. But you can't plead innocent if you've got it on you."
>—LOUISE LASSER, on her cocaine bust, 1976

"I really am a manifestation of my own fantasy."
>—SYLVESTER STALLONE, 1982

"I'm perhaps the most gifted actor of my generation."
>—DAVID CARRADINE, 1977

"Unfortunately, narcissism has gotten a bad name."
> —JOHN RECHY, 1978, author of *City of Night* (1963) and *Sexual Outlaw* (1977)

"The children and I have our life together now, and we're making it a glorious life."
> —JOAN CRAWFORD, in a fan-magazine article, after her divorce from Phillip Terry, 1946

"I was born with a Karma and what I make of this life will put me closer to God in the next. My ultimate goal is to become a saint."
> —MARISA BERENSON, 1976

"I thought I could be spokesman for my generation, for the millions of people under twenty-five who have no voice at all in the policies of this country or the progress of the world."
> —MIA FARROW, after months of meditation in India with the Maharishi Mahesh Yogi, 1968

"I tried everything. I tried *est*, Gestalt, grass. And then I found metaphysics."
> —DYAN CANNON

"I'm a practicing nothing. I have strong rapport with the Lord."
> —BARBARA HOWAR, 1976

"It is too early for a Polish Pope."
> —KAROL CARDINAL WOJTYLA (Pope John Paul II), a few days before he got the job, 1978

"Where my head is at now, expanding sexuality is not most satisfied through promiscuity but through continuously communicating with someone specifically."
> —JACK NICHOLSON, 1972

"It's not that Klein is too Jewish, just too German."

> —Barbi Benton, 1970, on why she allowed her lover, Hugh Hefner, to change her name from Klein

"This is the first time in nine centuries that we have Jewish blood [Diane's parents are Jewish]. But Jews are clever and shrewd and the little boy will need that. I came to their wedding but not to the reception. Eddie [Egon] understood. He sent a girl to my room."

> —Prince Tassilo von Fürstenberg, on the wedding of his son, Prince Egon, to Diane, 1973

"I cannot believe that these pagan countries, that have held back civilization for thousands of years, that have spent an eternity in the marketplaces smoking strange weeds and eating goat doodle, are the friends of modern democracy."

> —George Jessel, on Egypt and several other Arab countries

"I'm the only sane one in the family."

> —Billy Carter, to a TV interviewer

"I'm so against smoking that if some woman is at my table and she reaches for matches, I let her light the cigarette herself."

> —Tony Curtis, as chairman of the American Cancer Society's "I Quit" campaign, March 1969

"Smoking tobacco's got nothing to do with smoking marijuana. It's tobacco that gives you lung cancer."

> —Tony Curtis, in an interview with Earl Wilson, after he was fined for carrying pot in London in April 1970

"Elvis is so straight it's unbelievable. He doesn't swear or drink or smoke or anything like that. He could be President."

> —Peter Fonda, September 1970

"The advertisers are having a disastrous effect on every art they touch. They are not only seducing the artist, they are drafting him. They are not only drawing on him, they are sucking the soul out of him."
—ORSON WELLES, 1967

"Underneath, and not far underneath, I'm *too* gentle. I need tenderness and understanding as much as any woman, maybe more."
—RONA BARRETT, in her autobiography, 1974

"Keith and me are just like people in the street."
—MICK JAGGER, on Keith Richard, 1977

"Mostly it was like fried eggs but with no frying pan."
—SALVADOR DALÍ, asked for his recollections of the womb, 1964

"She shows signs of a beauty that will probably come with maturity."
—*Women's Wear Daily,* on Princess Anne of Great Britain, 1970

"All the Kennedy girls feel she [Joan] is the ideal wife, never ruffled, never complaining. She's good for Ted; calms him down. A terribly devoted couple."
—JEAN KENNEDY SMITH, on her sister-in-law, in "What It's Like to Marry a Kennedy," by Betty Hannah Hoffman, *Ladies' Home Journal,* October 1962

"Ted's a considerate person, especially to women."
—JOAN KENNEDY

"Being a fashion leader is at the very bottom of the things I desire."
—JACQUELINE KENNEDY, quoted by Igor Cassini

"A newspaper reported that I spend $30,000 a year buy-ing Paris clothes and that women hate me for it. I couldn't spend that much unless I wore sable underwear."

> —JACQUELINE KENNEDY, 1960. However, upon receiving a not unusual $40,000 clothing bill for his wife, JFK commented, "Is there such a thing as Shoppers Anonymous?"

"I don't have any money. I have exactly $5,200 in a bank account."

> —JACQUELINE KENNEDY ONASSIS to a friend, 1971

"She's a big nothing."

> —EVANGELIA KALOGEROPOULOS, mother of Maria Callas, on Jacqueline Onassis, 1971

"Lee is probably the most pure man I have ever known in my entire life. That's why I have to sue him."

> —MICHELLE TRIOLA MARVIN

"I certainly do not believe that Princess Margaret has done anything to give the Royal Family a bad name, as suggested. I am a loyal and obedient servant of the Queen."

> —RODDY LLEWELLYN, young friend of Princess Margaret, denying that his liaison with her was worthy of criticism.

"My life is a crystal teardrop."

> —JOAN BAEZ, in her autobiography, 1968

"This is the price you pay for being a media success."

> —STEVE RUBELL, 1979, owner of the popular Manhattan disco Studio 54, after pleading guilty to tax-evasion charges. Reminded that his first-year taxes were an unbelievably low $8,000, Rubell commented, "Now you're trying to turn it into a moral issue."

"The hard thing is when you have to dream up tasteless things to do on your own."
  —ANDY WARHOL, 1975

"I have a wonderful concept of the President. He'll kill me when I say it, but it's almost a fatherly love. That's how I think of him."
  —MARTHA MITCHELL, 1970

"He thought the book was very funny and entertaining."
  —MARGARET TRUDEAU, about her husband and her autobiography, 1979

"I have not read it."
  —PIERRE TRUDEAU, 1979

"He gave me half of his paycheck after taxes and felt that should be fine. Well, that only turned out to be $1,400 a month. I've got extravagant tastes for beautiful things, so that hardly paid for the children's Lacoste T-shirts."
  —MARGARET TRUDEAU, on the poor understanding her estranged husband had of money, 1982

"I wanted to be Helen Hayes with beautiful small roles. I just never thought about this kind of gaudy success."
  —LONI ANDERSON, on success, 1981

"I am used to grief. This is just a trifle."
  —ROMAN POLANSKI, asked by reporters how he felt about his arrest for the rape of a thirteen-year-old girl in Hollywood, 1977

"If this picture is just an attempt to capitalize on the name of Guevara and make a lot of money, then it's criminal, and I'd be sorry to have been associated with it."
  —JACK PALANCE, on his appearance as Fidel Castro in *Che* (1969)

"What has riding a subway got to do with reality? That's only something people do 'cause they don't have much money."

> —MICK JAGGER, asked by a German reporter if he ever made direct contact with his public by traveling in the subway, 1982

"They've done a lot of charity work."

> —DEBORAH HARRY of Blondie, on why she signed a lucrative endorsement contract with Murjani jeans, 1980

"The problem with writing is that there's not much money in it."

> —CHERYL TIEGS, after negotiating a $70,000-plus-royalties deal with Simon & Schuster to collaborate on a book

"I'd really like to travel again—anywhere but Italy. There's too much kidnapping there."

> —PATTY HEARST

"It has never been my nature to be competitive. . . ."

> —LAUREN BACALL, *Women's Wear Daily*, April 11, 1974

"Really, no one's gonna believe it, but John's a simple man with simple tastes. . . ."

> —CHRISTINA FERRARE, top model and wife of John De-Lorean, 1974

"Ma'am, ah'm not tryin' to be sexy. Ah didn't have any idear of trying to sell sex. It's just my way of expressin' how I feel when I move around. It's all leg movement. Ah don't do nothin' with my body."

> —ELVIS PRESLEY, to a reporter

"A little bit of rape is good for a man's soul."

> —NORMAN MAILER, in a speech at the University of California, Berkeley, 1972

"This young man is merely a disgruntled former employee. He acted as a chauffeur in my show."

> —LIBERACE, of the multimillion-dollar palimony suit filed against him by former employee Scott Thorson, 1982. Thorson and the entertainer, together for many years, had undergone plastic surgery to make themselves look alike.

"How far out it is to be a bird and fly around the trees. I am what I've always wanted to be and that is the truth. And I think—in fact, it's not what I think, but I observe that if people were to really take a good look at themselves, they are exactly the way they have always wanted to be. . . . My experience is that if I can tell you the truth, just lay it out there, then I have totally opened up a space for you to be who you are and that it really opens up all the room in the world for us to do whatever we want to do in regard to each other. If I don't like you, I'll tell you, and that's great."

> —JOHN DENVER

"I epitomize America."

> —JOHN DENVER

"I think that once you see emotions from a certain angle you can never think of them as real again."

> —ANDY WARHOL

"I know only that what is moral is what you feel good after and what is immoral is what you feel bad after."

> —ERNEST HEMINGWAY, *Death in the Afternoon* (1932)

"I'm so healthy I expect to live on and on."

> —J. I. RODALE, health publisher, while taping a 1971 *Dick Cavett Show;* he dropped dead moments after making this remark.

"I want blacks to feel that they are part of this country's existence. They are as much welcome at Buckingham Palace as anywhere else."
>—PRINCE CHARLES, 1982

"Everybody loves me, everybody loves me, but the only one I want to love me is you."
>—WAYNE NEWTON, ending a TV special singing to his horse, 1982

"What's the Mafia? I don't know anything about any Mafia."
>—FRANK SINATRA

ORDINARY
PEOPLE

"Goodness knows the trunk is big enough. It's big enough for two."

> —FRANK THOMPSON of South Africa, on why it was permissible for him to transport his servant around in the trunk of his car

"The American revolution was not a 'revolution.'"

> —Resolution passed by the California Bicentennial Commission, 1976

"Why can't he die like a man?"

> —DAVID SHIMP, on refusing to donate to his cousin the twenty-one ounces of bone marrow that might have saved his life

"They didn't ask me where I lived, they only asked me for an address."

> —GUSTAF RODING, a New Yorker, when questioned in court as to why he gave a wrong address when registering to vote

"America never did anything for me."
>—WILLIAM HENRY NELSON, defecting to Cuba, 1963

"Cuba didn't do anything for me either."
>—WILLIAM HENRY NELSON, returning to the U.S. on an inner-tube raft, 1968

"The D.A.R. [Daughters of the American Revolution] is appealing to young moderns."
>—MRS. MARION MONCURE DUNCAN, assuming the presidency of the DAR, 1962

"Except for the bothersome flies and mosquitoes, the smells issuing from the beach where gutted fish are allowed to rot in the sun and the humidity under which the village suffers most of the year, Chimo is the sort of idyllic paradise for which so many search."
>—SPENCER MURRAY and RALPH POOLE, *Power Boating the West Coast of Mexico*

"I had planned a career in teaching blind children—in fact, this is what I was actually doing before I regained my sight. But somehow, I felt that I wasn't as good a teacher after I could see again—and I became a [Playboy] Bunny."
>—CANDY LOBO, checkroom Bunny at the Kansas City Playboy Club, 1965. She was blind from age four to age seventeen when an operation restored her sight.

"I did it for Rice and the Rice community."
>—PENNY JOHNSON, on why she and a male student had appeared nude in the Rice University yearbook, 1969

"Why should I worry? He knows what he's doing."
>—MRS. SHIPWRECK KELLY. Her spouse, the great flagpole sitter, sat on a flagpole atop New York's Paramount Hotel for thirteen days, thirteen hours, and thirteen minutes in 1928.

"He's not dangerous at all; his family has been in captivity for eight generations."

>—ANTONIA, a Dutch model who shared her Paris flat with a
>pet panther, 1967

"I couldn't tell. They were wearing masks."

>—An Atlanta bus driver, queried about the sexual identity
>of streakers who invaded his bus in 1974

"It is impossible for the drivers to keep their timetable if they have to stop for passengers."

>—Response of a British bus company to complaints from
>passengers that drivers were speeding past lines of up to
>thirty people. "Get rid of the people and the system runs
>fine," the company also commented.

"We wanted to make them look better."

—Three South African farmers, charged with cruelty to animals after forcing milk into cows' udders with a bicycle pump, 1971

"Shut up, I am busy."

—Wireless operator on the *Titanic,* in a message to the S.S. *California* an hour before the tragedy. The *California* had wired that it was blocked by ice and the *Titanic* might also be in danger.

MEDIA

"He who attacks the fundamentals of the American [broadcasting] system attacks democracy itself."
> —WILLIAM S. PALEY, chairman of the board, CBS

"A program in which a large part of the audience is interested is by that very fact . . . in the public interest."
> —FRANK STANTON, president, CBS, 1955

"Radio has no future."
> —WILLIAM THOMSON, LORD KELVIN, president of the Royal Society (1890–95)

"I've often wondered how CBS could have . . . let me go on the air with no experience."
> —Newspaperwoman SALLY QUINN, blaming CBS for the inadequacies of her brief career as a morning TV co-host

"Television won't last. It's a flash in the pan."
> —MARY SOMERVILLE, pioneer in educational radio, 1948

"I don't want to be quoted, and don't quote me that I don't want to be quoted."

> —CBS correspondent WINSTON BURDETT, on the 1948 murder of correspondent George Polk

"The problem with television is that the people must sit and keep their eyes glued to a screen: the average American family hasn't time for it."

> —*The New York Times,* March 1939

"[The reason *Police Squad!* didn't work was that] it required constant viewing, and I don't think that people can watch a TV series without some distractions."

> —TONY THOMOPOULOS, president of ABC Entertainment, on why the series went under, 1982

"Circulation has reached an all-time high, and *Penthouse* has surpassed *Playboy* to become the biggest-selling men's magazine in the world. The reason? Respect! The respect *Penthouse* has for its readers; for their taste, attitudes, and personal opinions; for their privacy; and, above all, for their intelligence."

> —*Penthouse* "Housecall" column, August 1977

"I figured I had seen such injustice in my own life, that I'd been fucked around so often, that I might as well fuck other people. And I needed the money."

> —AL GOLDSTEIN, editor of *Screw* magazine, defending his earlier career as a company fink for the Bendix Corporation

"She's *too* sexy."

> —DORE SCHARY, turning down a suggestion that Marilyn Monroe be placed under contract at MGM

"I could smell it as the postman came whistling down the lane. Don't put a dime in it."

> —ROBERT BENCHLEY, advising John Hay Whitney not to invest in the play *Life with Father*. *Father* opened in 1939, became a hit, and ran for seven and a half years.

"Pass on it, Louis. Civil War pictures have never made a dime."

> —IRVING THALBERG, advising his boss, Louis B. Mayer, to pass on the film rights to *Gone With the Wind*

"Francis, as president of Paramount pictures, I must tell you that under no circumstances will Marlon Brando appear in *The Godfather*. And, as president, I no longer wish to waste the company's time even discussing it."

> —STANLEY JAFFE, president of Paramount Pictures, to *Godfather* director Francis Ford Coppola, according to Coppola

"I love the violence. I love the executions—I think they are tastefully done."

> —ROBERT CONRAD, on his 1977 martial-arts flick, *Sudden Death*

"We should distinguish between the two kinds of violence. If someone is violent toward those who seek freedom, that's bad. But if those who seek freedom use violence to achieve it, that's good."

> —MICHELANGELO ANTONIONI

"At its best, the American way of life is the best way of life, and American movies should reflect this."

> —NANCY REAGAN, 1980

"[The West created 007 to soften up the world for] the gas war in Vietnam, the murder of civil rights demonstrators in America and the blackmailing of young African nationalist states."
> —*Junge Welt,* East German community youth paper, on James Bond

"Paranoia is essential for preservation today."
> —STIRLING SILLIPHANT, screenwriter of *The Towering Inferno* (1974)

"It's all been a very chastening experience."
> —DAVID BEGELMAN, fired and then rehired as head of Columbia Pictures, after he stole more than $60,000 from the company over a two-year period, 1978

"I want to rule by love, not by fear."
> —LOUIS B. MAYER, founder of Metro-Goldwyn-Mayer, and one of the most hated men in Hollywood

"I lost honestly. . . . At no time was I coached or tutored. I have faith in the rest of the other contestants who were big money winners."
> —CHARLES VAN DOREN, 1959, denying charges he had won $129,000 unfairly on the *Twenty-one* TV quiz show. A short time later he admitted to having been coached by the show's producer in 1956 and 1957.

"It's enough to shake your faith in human nature."
> —CHARLES VAN DOREN

"The people who are trying to discredit me are ruthless, and they will stop at nothing. . . ."
> —CLIFFORD IRVING, author, miffed at allegations that his biography of Howard Hughes was a fake. It was.

"I'm certainly not trying to earn my living off the work of other people, I certainly can't blame my publishers, but I'm sad someone didn't bring this to my attention before."
> —LADY PAMELA HARLECH, whose cookbook, *Feast Without Fuss,* was found to have lifted 165 recipes straight from *Gourmet* magazine, 1977

"I'm sure the situation he finds himself in now is one of those things that could happen to any one of us. . . ."
> —Producer HOWARD KOCH, defending director Roman Polanski to the judge trying him for the statutory rape of a young girl

"People think of 'exploitation' as an evil word, but it's not. It just means taking a product and building it up."
> —SAMUEL Z. ARKOFF, "King of the B Pictures," producer of *The Amityville Horror* and *Beach Blanket Bingo*

"The tragic thing is that I drew the assignment because I am black."
> —WILLIAM MARSHALL, on having to take the title role in the blacksploitation movie *Blacula* (1972)

"I think *The Swarm* is going to be the most terrifying movie ever made."
> —IRWIN ALLEN, "Master of Disaster," producer of *The Poseidon Adventure* (1972) and *The Towering Inferno* (1974). Warner Bros. spent $6 million advertising the truly disastrous *Swarm,* which was described by *The New York Times* as "the surprise comedy hit of the season."

"People are going to see it in drive-ins and neighborhood nowhere theaters and they're going to be moved by it. People who were never moved by this story before. People who always thought that Jesus Christ was some kind of schmuck. They're going to see something beautiful and

they're going to cry. They won't be able to help themselves. When you really come to think of it, we're doing
Him a favor."

> —Director NORMAN JEWISON, on his movie *Jesus Christ
> Superstar* (1973)

"I get really offended when people compare it with *Jaws*.
It's going to make that movie look like an anemic sprat
alongside it. It's enormous in the true meaning of the
word. Enormous and truly grand and majestic and beautiful."

> —RICHARD HARRIS, of his unfortunate starring vehicle,
> *Orca*, of which the *Los Angeles Times* said: "A lousier movie
> may get made one of these months or years, but it will
> have to wrest the trophy from . . . *Orca*."

"In making this film, MGM feels privileged to add something of permanent value to the cultural treasure house of
mankind. . . ."

> —Publicity tag line for the film *Quo Vadis?* (1951)

"Henry, you've handled problems bigger in size, but not
bigger in emotion."

> —Producer BOB EVANS, responding to Henry Kissinger's
> offer to help him with the break-up of his marriage to Ali
> McGraw

"Color and stereoscopy will make the cinema into the
greatest art in the world. Bad films will be impossible."

> —JOHN BETJEMAN, 1935

"All my shows are great. Some of them are bad. But they
are all great."

> —LORD GRADE, 1975

"Who the hell wants to hear actors talk?"

> —H. M. WARNER, date unknown

MILITARY

"I've lived under situations where every decent man de-
clared war first, and I've lived under situations where you
don't declare war. We've been flexible enough to kill people
without declaring war."
> —LIEUTENANT GENERAL LEWIS B. HERSHEY, head of Se-
> lective Service, 1968

"Suppose the colonies do abound in men, what does that
signify? They are raw undisciplined cowardly men. . . .
Believe me, my Lords, the very sound of a cannon would
carry them off . . . as fast as their feet could carry them."
> —LORD SANDWICH, First Lord of the Admiralty, arguing in
> Parliament on the ease of putting down the American re-
> bellion, 1775

"You always write it's bombing, bombing, bombing. It's
not bombing. It's air support."
> —COLONEL H. E. OPFER, air attaché at the United States
> Embassy in Pnom-Penh, on the war in Vietnam

"There seems to be something wrong with our bloody ships today."

> —Attributed to SIR DAVID BEATTY, British admiral, on the sinking of British battlecruisers at the Battle of Jutland, 1916

"[We tried] to find out how we could continue doing what we were doing but report it accurately . . . [but] we couldn't find a way."

> —GENERAL JOHN D. LAVELLE, head of the Seventh Air Force in Vietnam, explaining to a congressional committee how his 400 fighter-bombers had bombed North Vietnam at least 147 times without authorization between November 1971 and March 1972

"Many people today see professional soldiers as the scum of the earth. The Green Berets are considered killers and baby eaters. But it's just like any other job that requires intensive training."

> —KEITH NELSON, professional soldier in Rhodesia who lost his legs there, 1978

"War has always been a part of Judeo-Christian history. Emphasis is on killing the soldiers in the battlefield and saving the cities. The neutron bomb is in the best interests of Judeo-Christian morality."

> —SAM COHEN, inventor of the neutron bomb

"War is killing people. When you kill enough people, the other side quits."

> —GENERAL CURTIS LEMAY, to a Rand Corporation physicist

"[Bombs are] aimed exclusively at military targets. Unfortunately, there are some civilians around these targets."
—Dwight D. Eisenhower, defending U.S. bombing tactics in North Vietnam

"I'd like to say that recruit depots are open to anyone, at anytime. Visitors can walk in and watch training or look up an individual they know. Sure, you can see people get tired running and fall down by the side of the road. But they do that practicing for the high school football team, too."

—GENERAL LOUIS H. WILSON, Marine Corps commandant of boot camps, defending the training after a recruit died in March 1976 as the result of a beating during a mock bayonet drill

"They're asking women to do impossible things. I don't believe women can carry a pack, live in a foxhole, or go a week without a bath."

—GENERAL WILLIAM WESTMORELAND, contemplating women in the armed services

"We are ready to step in the batter's box and belt a few pitches with hard stuff now that the contract is signed for our third season with the big leagues."

—COMMANDER JAMES CANNOR, captain of the U.S. destroyer *Mullinix*, returning his ship to Vietnam for its third tour of duty, 1972

"Come see the light at the end of the tunnel."

—Invitations for the New Year's Eve party at the American Embassy in Saigon, 1967

"The indices in Vietnam are good."

—WILLIAM F. BUCKLEY, 1970

"A lot of kids don't care for me but I think most of them are people I don't know. . . ."

—LIEUTENANT GENERAL LEWIS B. HERSHEY, head of Selective Service, 1969

"The enemy is hurting very badly."

>—Secretary of State DEAN RUSK, on Vietnam, 1967.
American casualties for the next year would reach fifty
thousand.

"As the U.S. Government has frequently stated, we seek
no wider war."

>—White House announcement, February 7, 1965. As it was
made, armored bombers were crossing the border of
North Vietnam.

"We have not widened the war. To the contrary, we have
shortened it."

>—Secretary of Defense MELVIN LAIRD to the National Se-
curity Council, February 9, 1971, as U.S. bombers were
accompanying South Vietnamese forces into Laos for the
first time

"Winding down the war."

>—RICHARD NIXON, on Vietnam. According to Daniel Ells-
berg, he dropped more bombs than Lyndon Johnson and
more than any head of state in history up to that time.

"I never thought of myself as a spy. I just flew an air-
plane."

>—FRANCIS GARY POWERS, whose spy plane was shot down
over Russia in May 1960

"Most observers now rate the 100,000 man South Korean
army as the best of its size in Asia. Its fast-moving columns
have mopped up all but a few of the Communist guerrilla
bands ... and no one believes that the Russian trained
North Korean army could pull off a quick, successful invasion of the south without heavy reinforcements."

>—*Time* magazine, in early June 1950—a few weeks before
the North Korean invasion of South Korea on June 25,
1950

"Military strength is most successful if it is never used. But if we are never to use force, we must be prepared to use it, and to use it successfully."
 —Secretary of Defense CASPAR WEINBERGER, 1982

"I guess we'll get through with them in one day."
 —GENERAL GEORGE ARMSTRONG CUSTER, after a scout reported he would find enough Sioux at Little Big Horn to keep up fighting for two or three days

"You can't beat short tours for boosting spirit in a war like this, especially when the short tours themselves are broken by a five-day free vacation to some exotic place like Hawaii or Hong Kong or Tokyo."
 —MAJOR GENERAL ORMOND SIMPSON, on the advantages of serving in Vietnam, 1969

"These sorts of things will happen in war."

> —GENERAL RICHARD AIREY, commenting on the carnage resulting from the charge of the Light Brigade (October 25, 1854). It was he who, under instructions from a superior, had given the order for the attack.

"Only war heightens all human energies to maximum tension and impresses a seal of nobility on the peoples who have the virtue to undertake it."

> —BENITO MUSSOLINI, 1932

"I cannot conceive of any use that the fleet will ever have for aircraft. . . . Aviation is just a lot of noise."

> —ADMIRAL CHARLES BENSON, chief of naval operations after W.W. I, responding to Billy Mitchell's plea that the navy make greater use of airplanes

"You will be home before the leaves have fallen from the trees."

> —KAISER WILHELM II, addressing troops leaving for the front, August 1914

"In three weeks England will have her neck wrung like a chicken."

> —GENERAL MAXIME WEYGAND, after the fall of France in 1940

"The noblest virtues of man are developed in war. Without war the world would degenerate and disappear in a morass of materialism."

> —FIELD MARSHAL HELMUTH VON MOLTKE

"We had to destroy it in order to save it."

> —An American officer explaining to an AP reporter the destruction of the Vietnamese city of Ben Tre

"The My Lai operation was briefed for visitors as one of our successful operations."
> —COLONEL ORAN K. HENDERSON, brigade commander in Vietnam, whose troops killed between 102 and 347 men, women, and children in the village of My Lai, March 16, 1968

"Personally, I didn't kill any Vietnamese that day: I mean personally. I represented the United States of America. My country."
> —LIEUTENANT WILLIAM C. CALLEY, the only military person found guilty of the murders at My Lai

"I can't believe an American serviceman would purposely shoot any civilian; any atrocities in this war were caused by the Communists."
> —GEORGE WALLACE, on the atrocities in the Vietnamese village of Son My

"We don't give the Phalangists orders, and we're not responsible for them."
> —LIEUTENANT GENERAL RAFAEL EYTAN, Israeli Chief of Staff, of the massacres in the Sabra and Shatila refugee camps, Beirut, September 15–18, 1982

"A bomb carried by a boy on a bicycle or mortar shells fired at Danang base just three days ago are just as much bombs as those carried by planes to the North."
> —Secretary of State DEAN RUSK, explaining to the House Foreign Affairs Committee why bombs delivered via bicycle were just as powerful as the six-ton bombloads carried by Phantom jets, 1965

"By war alone can we acquire those virile qualities necessary to win the stern strife of actual life."
> —THEODORE ROOSEVELT

"Don't knock the war that feeds you."
>—Slogan on the wall of a West Coast defense plant during the Vietnam war

"I do not contend that driving people crazy, even briefly, is a pleasant prospect. But to those who feel that *any* kind of chemical weapon is more horrible than conventional weapons, I put this question: Would you rather be *temporarily* deranged, blinded or paralyzed by a chemical agent—or burned alive by a conventional fire bomb?"
>—MAJOR GENERAL WILLIAM M. CREASY, on "psychochemical warfare," 1957

"The most perfect shape, the sublimest image that has been recently created in Germany has not come out of any artist's studio. It is the steel helmet."
>—S.S. officer COUNT BAUDISSIN, 1930s

In 1930, young GENERAL DOUGLAS MACARTHUR wanted to become Chief of Staff. His boss, Secretary of War Patrick J. Hurley, had just sent a routine message on the Philippines to the Senate. Seeing an opportunity, MacArthur sent Hurley the following:

> "It is the most comprehensive and statesmanlike paper that has ever been presented with reference to this complex and perplexing problem. At one stroke it has clarified issues which have perplexed and embarrassed statesmen for the last thirty years. If nothing else had ever been written upon the subject, your treatise would be complete and absolute. . . . It is the most statesmanlike utterance that has emanated from the American Government in many decades. . . ."

Note: It worked! MacArthur received his promotion on August 6, 1930.

"The Russians might attack Washington, but I'll be damned if they'd be insane enough to attack Texas."

> —REAR ADMIRAL ROBERT Y. KAUFMAN, attempting to defuse Texan fears of an underground ultra-low-frequency-signal transmitting system proposed for the state, 1975

"I'd go in there tomorrow and be a guinea pig and sit in a foxhole right under one of those bombs if they'd give me a discharge."

> —Marine RALPH GONZALEZ of New York, explaining how close he was prepared to go to an exploding atomic bomb, 1952

"As far as sinking a ship with a bomb is concerned, you just can't do it."

> —REAR ADMIRAL CLARK WOODWARD, 1939

"A grossly overrated weapon."

> —SIR DOUGLAS HAIG, British field marshal during World War I, on the machine gun

"Actual performance exceeds both the contractor's proposed performance and his contractual commitments by nearly one percent (both of which exceeded Air Force expectations by seven percent) and in no single characteristic is there a deficiency."

> —Assistant Secretary of the Air Force ROBERT H. CHARLES, extolling the Lockheed C-5A airplane to a Senate committee in 1969. Actually, the C-5A was an unmitigated disaster, costing the government $2 billion in overruns because of deficiencies. The first C-5A, for example—greeted by President Johnson as it came off the assembly line—looked complete but was actually missing more than three thousand parts; later, it blew up.

"There are also enough rocks on earth to kill the world's population several times over."

> —LIEUTENANT GENERAL DANIEL GRAHAM, former director of the Defense Intelligence Agency, defending the over-accumulation of nuclear weapons, 1982

Secretary of Defense Melvin Laird: "I've tried to be as forthcoming on information about our activities and the use of air power in Cambodia as I possibly could. . . . I just don't believe that anyone can find a case where I've shied away, have not given you complete and full information. . . . If there is a problem of some information that you don't have, that you want, I hope you'll ask me and I hope you'll ask me right now, 'cause I'm willing to answer those questions."

Question: "How many sorties are we flying in a day?"

Laird: "The number of sorties is a matter which I have not released, and we are not releasing the sortie levels."

> —Secretary of Defense MELVIN LAIRD, September 2, 1970, meeting with reporters covering the Pentagon

ECONOMICS

"There has been a little distress selling on the Stock Exchange."

> —THOMAS W. LAMONT, senior partner of Morgan Trust
> Company, October 24, 1929

"There is nothing in the business situation to justify any nervousness."

> —EUGENE M. STEVENS, president, Continental Illinois
> Bank, October 1929

"These really are good times but only a few know it."
> —*The New York Times,* 1931

"Meat costs what it costs because that's what it costs. All those people do all those things. They all get paid—and they all make a profit. If they didn't make a profit they wouldn't do what they do. And that would be bad."

> —From *Mary Mutton and the Meat Group,* a U.S. government
> pamphlet

"If you extrapolate the strains that we now already see as a consequence of what we have for an extended period of time, the institutions—economical, financial, structural—begin to break down because they are essentially constructed or have been developed over the decades in the context of low, simple-digit inflation. . . ."

> —ALAN GREENSPAN, chairman of President Ford's Council of Economic Advisers. James J. Kilpatrick, Jr., noted that Greenspan "speaks no English, and the rest of us speak no Greenspan."

"In all likelihood, world inflation is over."

> —Managing Director of the International Monetary Fund, 1959

"Men can be put to work and general prosperity will return only by enlisting the unemployed to create, under proper leadership, the desire to buy."

> —ROGER BABSON, economist, 1930s

"I do not think the United States is in a recession. We do have economic problems, but it's a very mixed situation."

> —GERALD FORD, 1974

"We may well be moving into a period where the rate of inflation is slowing down, not just on a temporary basis but perhaps on a more fundamental basis."

> —ALAN GREENSPAN, November 1974

"Unless drastic measures are taken to prevent it, the capitalist system throughout the civilized world will be wrecked within a year. I should like this prediction filed for future reference."

> —Private letter, attributed to GOVERNOR NORMAN of the Bank of England, to Governor Moret of the Bank of France, 1931

"The world economy hasn't really suffered owing to the increase in oil prices and has in fact recouped."
—Sheik Ahmad Zaki Yamani of Saudi Arabia, 1975

"A billion dollars here, a billion dollars there, and pretty soon you're talking about real money."
—Senator Everett Dirksen

"It is my judgment that our economy is neither in a depression or recession. I project slow growth [in the gross national product] in the last half of this year and into early 1975.... Unemployment may be, at the worst, six percent."

> —BERYL W. SPRINKEL, economist with Chicago's Harris Bank, predicting for 1974. By the end of that year interest rates had soared to new heights, the stock market had plunged 300 points, and the economy was sinking deeper into recession as prices rose.

"In the types of companies we are interested in the values are better than they have been in a long time."

> —DAVID BABSON, recommending the following stocks for purchase in 1974: Xerox (to fall 55 percent); Coca-Cola (to go down 65 percent); American Motors (down 60 percent); IBM (off 33 percent); Merck (down 20 percent); Proctor & Gamble (15 percent decline); Kodak (down 45 percent)

"The entire graduated-income-tax structure was created by Karl Marx."

> —RONALD REAGAN

THE GOOD EARTH

"The environment movement is one of the subversive element's last steps. They've gone after the military and the police and now they're going after our parks and playgrounds."

—MRS. CLARENCE HOWARD, delegate from Missouri to the seventy-ninth DAR Convention, on Earth Day, May 4, 1970

"Opponents of peacetime applications of 2, 4, 5-T have repeatedly launched false, malicious attacks on the safety of the product."

—Fact sheet put out by the Dow Chemical Company on the chemical used in Agent Orange, a defoliant spread by the air force in Vietnam. Investigation revealed that the manufacture of 2, 4, 5-T creates a poisonous by-product, dioxin, reportedly so toxic that three ounces could kill the population of New York City if poured into the water supply.

"Seen one redwood, you've seen 'em all."
—Ronald Reagan, on ecology

"Most of the chemicals are not a problem as far as adverse effects. . . . The stuff you smell isn't necessarily anything to worry about."
—Health commissioner of Niagara County, New York, reassuring residents of the Love Canal area

"The thing has been blown up out of context."
—Armand Hammer, chairman of the board of Occidental Petroleum, parent company of Hooker Chemical Company which had buried 22,000 tons of chemical refuse—including some of the most deadly substances known—in the Love Canal area

"DDT, the most effective pesticide, was outlawed on the theoretical grounds that it might someday, under some circumstances, harm someone. . . ."
>   —RONALD REAGAN, 1978

"It must have been impossible for our elders to imagine life in this land without the polluted air in which they lived—before people were liberated from the congested cities by the motor vehicle. There were reeking livery stables in every neighborhood. Cow barns were the customary auxiliaries to dairies. There were malodorous privies in every backyard. The dirt in the unpaved streets was . . . a fetid compound of filth. . . ."
>   —HARRY WILLIAMS, managing director of the American Manufacturers Association, on how the automobile had saved America from pollution, 1957

"Hydrochloric acid is the same acid contained in the human stomach."
>   —Spokesman for the Society of the Plastics Industry, on why plastic—which gives off hydrochloric acid when it is burned—could not be an environmental irritant

"Pollution takes many forms. In the American experience, by far the most damaging form has been stagnation. Economic stagnation."
>   —Mobil Oil Corporation ad in *The New York Times,* May 4, 1972

"We prefer economic growth to clean air."
>   —CHARLES BARDEN, executive director of the Texas Air Control Board

"Everything is under control. There is and was no danger to public health and safety. . . . No increase in normal radiation levels had been detected."

> —LIEUTENANT GOVERNOR WILLIAM SCRANTON, III, of Pennsylvania, in his first statement on the Three Mile Island incident, 1979

"There was nothing there that was catastrophic or unplanned for."

> —JOHN G. HERBEIN, vice-president for power generation of Metropolitan Edison, which owns the Three Mile Island plant, 1979

"[The film *China Syndrome*] hasn't any scientific credibility and is, in fact, ridiculous. *Syndrome* rendered an unconscionable public disservice by using phony theatrics to frighten Americans away from a desperately needed energy source."

> —An executive of Southern California Edison, a short time before the incident at Three Mile Island

"A nuclear power plant is infinitely safer than eating, because 300 people choke to death on food every year."

> —DIXY LEE RAY, governor of the state of Washington, 1977

"How do we know? Fallout might be good for us."

> —DR. EDWARD TELLER, father of the hydrogen bomb, responding to questions from Groucho Marx, 1950s

"Having created the atom bomb, the American imperialists began talking about creation of a hydrogen bomb. Our scientists, as the saying goes, put this in their pipes, wound it around their whiskers, worked a bit and created the hydrogen bomb *before* it was invented in the United States."

> —NIKITA KHRUSHCHEV, in a statement to agricultural workers, 1961

"We aren't afraid of atomic bombs. What if they killed even 300 million? We would still have plenty more. . . ."
—MAO ZEDONG, 1957

"Everyone agrees that a nuclear war could be an unparalleled disaster. But it need not be an *unmitigated* disaster."
—From a recent publication of the Federal Emergency Management Agency (FEMA)

"Atlanta was the first city in the United States to evacuate. They evacuated toward the end of the Civil War at the request of General Sherman. Some 10,000 people moved out of there. So, there's been an evacuation."
—VAL PETERSON, U.S. administrator of civil defense, citing evidence for the feasibility of evacuating American cities before an atomic attack, 1955

"Get out of town."
—VAL PETERSON, on the best thing to do when a city is under atomic attack

"Dig a hole, cover it with a couple of doors and then throw three feet of dirt on top. . . . It's the dirt that does it. . . . If there are enough shovels to go around, everybody's going to make it."
—T. K. JONES, deputy under secretary of defense for strategic and theater nuclear forces, on procedures to follow in the event of nuclear attack

"This postage-free card would be used by displaced survivors of an attack to notify the Postal Service of their emergency mailing addresses."
—U.S. Postal Service emergency-planning manual, describing plans for the distribution of Emergency Change of Address Cards after an atomic attack

RICH AND POOR

"I had the pay phone installed in my [country] place because I knew that guests preferred it that way. It saved them the trouble of settling with me afterward, or of attempting to pay for their phone calls. It saved them trouble. And yet a spate of letters and cartoons resulted. You might have thought I was pathologically inclined, instead of taking a simple, rational step."
        —J. Paul Getty, 1965

"The poor aren't any different from the rich—they just don't have as much money."
        —Senator S. I. Hayakawa of California

"The chief problem of the lower-income farmers is poverty."
        —Nelson Rockefeller

"Our Heavenly Father never sends us more mouths than He can feed."

> —HENRY M. GUERNSEY, *Plain Talks on Avoided Subjects* (1882)

"I just have faith that if through some sort of circumstances welfare did disappear tomorrow, no one would ever miss a meal. The people in this country . . . would get together, form emergency committees, and take up the slack."

> —RONALD REAGAN

"The White House really badly, badly needs china."

> —NANCY REAGAN, who ordered 220 new place settings for the White House at a cost of $209,508. The cost was covered by a private donor, 1981.

"You can say that this administration will have the first complete, far-reaching attack on the problem of hunger in history. Use all the rhetoric, so long as it doesn't cost money."

> —RICHARD NIXON, in the official minutes of a White House meeting, March 17, 1969

"Some people want champagne and caviar when they should have beer and hot dogs."

> —DWIGHT D. EISENHOWER, 1949

"I do not want to deprive any citizen of his or her spirit of self-reliance."

> —PATRICK J. HURLEY, Hoover's Secretary of War, arguing against a congressional proposal to establish a $100 million fund for relief, 1932

"Nobody, but nobody, has to be poor in this country. If I wasn't making movies, I could go out in the street and make $500 a week selling pencils."

> —JAMES CAAN, 1980

"Some people are always starving somewhere."
    —Secretary of Agriculture EARL T. BUTZ, sloughing off the
    world hunger crisis of 1974

"If I were convinced that by giving away my fortune I could make a real contribution toward solving the problems of world poverty, I'd give away 99.5 percent of all I have immediately."
    —J. PAUL GETTY, 1965

"The gaps [between rich and poor] aren't bad. They create a kind of void which exerts an upward situation. It's like the successive waves of immigrants in the United States and their changing upward economic roles. On a worldwide basis, this happens in much more complex ways but, in some ways, even more rapidly."
    —HERMAN KAHN, 1977

"Oh, all this talk about money. I find it *affreuse,* disgusting, hateful. I hate money, I never bother about money. What use is money, so long as you have enough to live well? The necessities. What's the use of having more?"

> —CAYETANA, DUCHESS OF ALBA, owner of at least sixty-three titles, more than fifty castles, and a collection of masterpieces beyond price, 1963

"A man who has a million dollars is as well off as if he were rich."

> —Attributed to JOHN JACOB ASTOR, III

"Harvey Firestone, III, went to Havana for a vacation trip. It is our feeling that inasmuch as he was capable of standing and walking, he might possibly have wheeled himself to the terrace and stood up to see the view, toppling over the low balcony."

> —LEONARD K. FIRESTONE and RAYMOND C. FIRESTONE, in a joint statement denying that their crippled nephew, Harvey Firestone, III, had taken his life. Firestone, who was in a wheelchair, jumped or fell from the twentieth floor of the Havana Hilton Hotel. Two months earlier, he had tried to jump from a speeding car.

"[The Depression] solved the eternal domestic service problem in America."

> —*Fortune* magazine, during the 1930s

"There's no more happiness with ten servants than with one."

> —MARYLOU WHITNEY (Mrs. Cornelius "Sonny" Vanderbilt Whitney)

"I'm sure there are people in Greenwich [Connecticut] who are glad there are illegal immigrants here, because they wouldn't have someone to help in the house without them."
> —PRESCOTT BUSH, brother of Vice-President George Bush, campaigning for the U.S. Senate in Connecticut, 1982

"Mrs. Burden, with the help of a maid, is learning how to keep house."
> —*Vogue* magazine on Amanda Burden in 1965, the year she and her husband, Carter, were singled out by the magazine as New York's perfect young couple

"She doesn't run her house. She creates it. The maids are charmed, the butler's dazzled. Everything is effortless and flexible . . . almost impromptu. And the children absolutely adore her."
> —*Harper's Bazaar,* describing Cristina Ford, August 1973

"[Saving energy] is my asking my servants not to turn on the self-cleaning oven until after seven in the evening."
> —BETSY BLOOMINGDALE, on her contribution to the energy crisis, 1981

"This is a way of doing something nice for poor little animals, with no political implications one way or another."
> —LARRY APODACA, defending the birthday party Michele Bertotti, a divorced New York City art collector, gave for her black Schipperke, Fellow, at the Animal Gourmet, a dog delicatessen on Manhattan's East Side. At the party, which was written up in *The New York Times,* guests dined on liver-paté canapés, shrimp on rye-bread rounds, beef ragout, steak tartare, Swedish meatballs, and, of course, doggie birthday cake.

"If you destroy the leisure class, you destroy civilization."
> —J. P. MORGAN

"I wake up at two, sometimes at three. First is my massage. Afterwards I answer my phone calls and see my bankers, racing managers and lawyers—the usual daily chores."

> —THE MAHARANEE OF BARODA, to Charlotte Curtis of *The New York Times*

"At three o'clock on Sunday afternoons everybody is playing polo."

> —A member of the DU PONT family, turning down an advertising agency's suggestion that he sponsor a Sunday afternoon radio program in the 1930s

"He's a magnificent man, but suppose some simpleminded schmucks take all that business about burning down buildings *seriously.*"

> —A comment in response to a talk by Ray "Masai" Hewitt, Black Panther minister of education, at a socialite party held for the Panthers by Sidney and Gail Lumet in 1969

"I've never met a Panther—this is a first for me!"

> —CHERAY (Mrs. Peter) DUCHIN, at Leonard Bernstein's socialite party for the Black Panthers, 1970. The party, which led to the coining of the term "radical chic," was to raise funds for twenty-one Panthers indicted for plotting to kill a policeman and dynamite a police station and department stores.

"This is a very paradoxical situation. Having this apartment makes this meeting possible, and if this apartment didn't exist, you wouldn't have it. And yet—well, it's a very paradoxical situation."

> —LEONARD BERNSTEIN, on the anomaly of having a fundraising party for the Panthers in his expensive apartment

"I worked for charity all my life, and now it's kind of fun to work for money."

> —CHARLOTTE FORD, daughter of Henry Ford, II

"It's something I've always wanted to do. I figured I can't ride horses *all* my life."

> —Debutante CORNELIA GUEST, of her new career as a model, 1982

"But then sometimes it is the help. Sometimes they say to me, 'Dr. Gucci, we used to have such aristocratic customers in here. . . . Now it is all those *boys* and so many Japanese,' and I tell my help that the Japanese are the aristocrats of customers. . . . They may not be very good-looking but right now they are the aristocrats."

> —ALDO GUCCI, owner of the ultra-snobbish store that bears his name, on the problems confronting his salespeople

"When my maid packed my bags, she said, 'Madame, some of these evening dresses have gone to Palm Beach with you three times.' I'm hoping nobody will remember."

> —THE DUCHESS OF WINDSOR, on how she had been skimping on clothes, 1966

"We don't think it fitting, to spend too much in these times."

> —PRINCE ALEXIS MDIVANI, cutting costs on a twenty-second birthday party for his wife, Barbara Hutton (1934). A modest little party in Paris cost $10,000 and included among the guests: two princes, one duchess, three barons, thirteen counts, one earl, and one hundred lesser folk.

"It's rude and inconsiderate to overtip. It only makes things difficult—and embarrassing—for people who are not as rich as I am."

> —J. PAUL GETTY

"Money does not grow on trees."

> —MARYLOU WHITNEY (Mrs. Cornelius "Sonny" Vanderbilt Whitney), in a note reprimanding her kitchen staff for the purchase of ham at $5 a pound, 1967

"God gave me my money."
         —JOHN D. ROCKEFELLER

"Mr. Jones is wrong to suggest that I support the rich against the poor. To the Christian there is no class distinction—that idea was largely concocted by the working classes."
         —Letter in the *Reynolds News* (England)

"You have helped us understand what it means to function in disaster and finish in style."

> —Dedication in the yearbook of the fashionable Madeira School to its headmistress, Jean Harris

"At the end, the acquisition of wealth is ignoble in the extreme. I assume that you save and long for wealth only as a means of enabling you the better to do some good in your day and generation."

> —ANDREW CARNEGIE

"The most patriotic thing I can do for my country is to remain solvent."

> —JAMES E. SINCLAIR, partner in Vilas and Hickey, a Wall Street firm, 1975

"I know all is lost. I'm going to enlist in the armed forces and ask for immediate duty in Vietnam."

> —ANDRÉ PORUMBEANU, learning that his ex-wife, heiress Gamble Benedict, had remarried, 1965. Porumbeanu was Benedict's chauffeur when they wed.

"I would like to ask those who were not amused if they seriously believe that as a result of that evening I have deprived one human being of one more mouthful of food. . . . I do not think it represents contempt for world hunger any more than if I had won the Mercedes-Benz that was put up for auction."

> —CRAIG CLAIBORNE, replying to readers of *The New York Times* who were irate about the $4,000 he and Pierre Franey spent on a thirty-one-course dinner in Paris in 1975. The pair bid $300 at a Channel 13 fund-raising auction for a dinner donated by American Express at any restaurant that accepted the American Express card. American Express, and thousands of others, were astonished when the restaurant chosen turned out to be in Paris.

EXPERT ADVICE

"Day by day in every way I am getting better and better."
— ÉMILE COUÉ, promoter of a fad that emphasized self-mastery by autosuggestion, 1923

"Put a big, broad, honest-to-God smile on your face; throw back your shoulders; take a good, deep breath; and sing a snatch of song. . . . If you can't sing, whistle. If you can't whistle, hum. You will quickly discover that it is physically impossible to remain blue or depressed while you are acting out the symptoms of being radiantly happy."
— DALE CARNEGIE

"Come on, women of America, let us smile. Let us work! Let us be cheerful-beautiful. Let us spend well and wisely. The crisis has passed. America is improving in health."
— ELIZABETH ARDEN, in a 1932 magazine article urging women to smile and spend their way out of the Depression

"Hold your thoughts on ... money by concentration, or fixation of attention, with your eyes closed, until you can actually see the physical appearance of money. Do this at least once a day."
> —NAPOLEON HILL, author of *The Law of Success* (1977) and *How to Sell Your Way Through Life*

"The essence of greatness is the ability to choose personal fulfillment in circumstances where others choose madness."
> —WAYNE W. DYER, *Your Erroneous Zones* (1976)

"Can you buy friendship? You not only can, but must. It's the *only* way to obtain friends. Everyone buys all his friends—in the Free-Enterprise Friendship Market."
> —ROBERT J. RINGER, *Looking Out for # 1* (1977)

"Spend all you can; never mind what your husband says; that is the best way to spread prosperity."
> —CHARLES M. SCHWAB, chairman of the board of Bethlehem Steel, advising married women to spend the nation back to economic health, 1931

"No illness is more simple to cure than cancer (this also applies to mental diseases and heart trouble) through a return to the most elementary natural eating and drinking: Diet No. 7."
> —GEORGE OHSAWA, *Zen Macrobiotics* (1965)

"We can cure homosexuality, drug addiction, alcoholism, psychosis, as well as endocrine disorders, headaches, stomach ulcers, asthma."
> —ARTHUR JANOV, *The Primal Scream* (1970)

"Your illness can confer substantial benefits. . . . An enforced holiday in bed blamelessly releases us from too busy a world, sharpens our mental and spiritual perceptions, permits a clearer perspective on our lives. An illness should be regarded as an opportunity to gather dividends and generate energies that mere health cannot possibly bestow."

> —DR. LOUIS E. BISCH, "Turn Your Sickness into an Asset,"
> *Reader's Digest,* November 1937

"Speaking of weight, one cup of black coffee with an oily meal has more fattening power than a glass of milk. The coffee turns against the oils in your food, and increases the energy potential of the meal."

> —DAN DALE ALEXANDER, best-selling health author of the 1950s

"If a mother wants a boy baby, she must bend her will to that effort, repeating with absolute confidence thirty or forty times a day, 'My child will be a boy!' If she intends him to be a great painter, she will insist on this to herself. She will visit art galleries and surround herself with beauty, and above all she will think beautiful things."

> —ÉMILE COUÉ, 1920s

"Try to make the officer feel important by talking about the danger and difficulty of his job. Portray yourself as a law-abiding citizen, an average working person beset by problems. When he returns to your excessive speed, say, 'Gee, I'm sorry. I didn't realize that . . . It was just that I was thinking about . . .' Here, you recount a unique personal dilemma that you confide in him. Everyone has something: a tyrannical boss, a sick spouse, an aged and arthritic parent, an installment payment that can't be met, an unfaithful mate, or a disappointing child."

> —HERB COHEN, on talking your way out of a speeding ticket, in *You Can Negotiate Anything* (1980)

"Little affairs [may be useful for many reasons, including] the opportunity to replace lovers who have contributed sexual dissonance with others more able to contribute consonance."

> —JEAN BAER, *How to Be an Assertive (Not Aggressive) Woman* (1976)

"Always do it in the daytime, because at night your heart takes over. Take her to lunch, to a very chic place like Le Pavillon or The Colony, where she will see famous people and where it is against the rules to scream or throw the crockery. Buy her a drink, and then tell her that the train has reached Chicago and you're getting off at Chicago. Tell her she's the most wonderful woman you've ever known. Then buy her a great lunch, and let her absorb the news as she eats. Afterward, you can walk out into the sunshine a free man. It never fails."

> —JIM AUBREY, on how to leave your lover. Aubrey was president of CBS for five years until fired in February 1965.

"The only reason people give me money is because they want me to have it, because they love me."

> —LEONARD ORR, founder and guru of "Theta" Rebirthing seminars which emphasize pursuing self-interest and the accumulation of capital

"*You,* as a person, never rate as bad, no matter how mistaken your sex acts. If you get women pregnant, your *behavior* certainly seems stupid and antisocial. But *you* cannot legitimately get labeled as hopelessly stupid or antisocial, since, as a result of this experience, you may change tomorrow and most scrupulously employ contraceptive techniques."

> —ALBERT ELLIS, *Sex and the Liberated Man* (1976)

"I do it because I do it, because that's what I do."

> —WERNER ERHARD, on why he developed *est*

"You've been taught that going to the dentist is a nasty experience, and one that is associated with pain. . . . But these are all learned reactions. You could make the whole experience work for rather than against you by choosing to make it a pleasant, exciting procedure. You could, if you really decided to use your brain, make the sound of the drill signal a beautiful sexual experience and each time the brrrrrrr sound appeared, you could train your mind to envision the most orgiastic moment of your life."
　　—WAYNE W. DYER

"The mind trains with drugs. It acquires new reflexes, a new kind of coordination. It exercises its muscles and gets itself ready to take the leap into the future."
　　—ROBERT HUNTER, *The Storming of the Mind* (1971)

"The woman who finds pleasure in cleaning actually enjoys the physical work involved. She gives herself to the task graciously and her movements are relaxed and rhythmical."
　　—ALEXANDER LOWEN, founder of "Bioenergetics"

"I can help many of these people. It depends on the psychic atmosphere and whether God really·wants them to know."
　　　—JEANE DIXON, of those who come to her for stock-market advice

"If everyone's barriers were broken down through therapy, it would be much easier to meet people. If all the people in Russia and America were psychoanalyzed, world politics would be a lot different. And better."
　　　—JAN ORANGE, a single woman quoted in "Being Single in New York" by Susan Dietz, *New York Post*, July 5, 1977

"Turn on, tune in and drop out."
　　—TIMOTHY LEARY, on his new religion based on LSD, 1966

POLITICS

"The merit of this gentleman is certainly great, and I heartily wish that fortune may distinguish him as one of her favorites. I am convinced that he will do everything that his prudence and valor shall suggest to add success to our arms."
— GEORGE WASHINGTON, on Benedict Arnold

"I think our government is honestly and economically managed."
— ULYSSES S. GRANT, in the midst of his presidency (1869–1877), one of the most corrupt, bribe-ridden and plunder-prone eras in U.S. history

"When more and more people are thrown out of work, unemployment results."
— CALVIN COOLIDGE

"Not heroics but healing, not nostrums but normalcy, not revolution but restoration, not agitation but adjustment, not surgery but serenity, not the dramatic but the dispassionate, not experiment but equipoise, not submergence in internationality but sustainment in triumphant nationality."

> —WARREN G. HARDING, 1921

"You know that your future is still ahead of you."

> —THOMAS E. DEWEY, in the 1948 presidential campaign

"Let us begin by committing ourselves to the truth, to see it like it is and to tell it like it is, to find the truth, to speak the truth and live with the truth. That's what we'll do."

> —RICHARD NIXON, nomination acceptance speech, August 8, 1968

"Did you bug that conversation?"
"No, Senator, I did not."
"What did you do?"
"I recorded it."

> —JOHN D. EHRLICHMAN, at the Watergate hearings

"If I do nothing else as President, I'm going to restore respect for the American flag."

> —RICHARD NIXON to Charles Colson, summer 1970

"When Ah get to the White House, you just come up to the gate, ring the bell, give your name, and Ah'm gonna let you in myself."

> —Senator ESTES KEFAUVER, in the 1956 primary for the Democratic nomination

"The great virtue of my radicalism lies in the fact that I am perfectly ready, if necessary, to be radical on the conservative side."

> —THEODORE ROOSEVELT to William Howard Taft, September 1906

"Even if he were mediocre, there are a lot of mediocre judges and people and lawyers, and they are entitled to a little representation, aren't they?"

> —Senator ROMAN HRUSKA, defending President Nixon's nomination of G. Harrold Carswell to the Supreme Court, 1970

"I only contribute to candidates who can't be bought."
>—CLINT MANGES, South Texas rancher-oilman, explaining his contributions of $900,000 to the Democratic primary, 1983

"I always enjoy the company of political figures and that happens to be my hobby."
>—TONGSUN PARK, lobbyist for South Korea, and influence peddler, after he was indicted on a political payoff scheme, bribery, illegal campaign contributions, mail fraud, racketeering, and failure to register as an agent of the Korean Central Intelligence Agency. Twenty-three congressmen and senators were also named in "Koreagate," August 1977.

"Some people have even said what I have done in Washington was mysterious, at least, and constituted illicit activities. But I want to tell you what I have done in Washington I like to say constituted an American success story on a small scale."
>—TONGSUN PARK, before the House Ethics Committee, April 3, 1978

"There's an honest graft, and I'm an example of how it works. I might sum up the whole thing by sayin' 'I seen my opportunities and took 'em. . . .' "
>—GEORGE WASHINGTON PLUNKITT, Tammany Hall leader, recorded by William Riordan, c. 1905

"I would have preferred not to take the money but I didn't want my own investigation to die."
>—Congressman RICHARD KELLY of Florida, who claimed he took $25,000 cash from Abscam agents because he himself was investigating them, 1980. Of the money that videotapes showed him stuffing into his pocket, the congressman said: "These people had the capacity to have me followed, and I wanted to demonstrate I was spending the money."

"The hell with it— They're not going to find anything."
> —Mayor JIMMY WALKER of New York, appearing before the Seabury investigating commission in 1932. The corruption unearthed by the commission forced Walker to resign.

"Everybody who knows me knows I have a very poor memory."
> —Former senator EDWARD GURNEY of Florida, unable to recall, on the witness stand, the campaign irregularities for which he was standing trial

"I certainly never intended to mislead anyone. Either they didn't listen carefully or I didn't express myself carefully."
> —BRUCE F. CAPUTO, a former congressman and a Republican candidate for U.S. senator from New York, who had described himself as a Vietnam-era "draftee" and an army lieutenant although he had been neither, February 1982. Caputo actually had held a civilian job in the Defense Department to avoid being drafted.

"The business of politics is symbolism."
> —JOHN LINDSAY, as reported by his press secretary, Tom Morgan

"I wouldn't know her if she was to fall on top of me."
> —Congressman JOHN DINGELL, denying any memory of the call girl allegedly procured for him, 1976

"I hired her because I felt sorry for her."
> —Congressman WAYNE HAYS of Ohio, on his so-called secretary and actual mistress, Liz Ray. Of her $14,000-a-year secretarial post, Ray confided: "I can't type, I can't file. I can't even answer the phone." The scandal destroyed Hays's powerful career; he resigned in August 1976.

"I like having a liberated wife."

> —Congressman JOHN JENRETTE, of his wife, Rita, 1978.
> They were divorced in 1981 after she found $25,000 in
> Abscam funds hidden in his shoe.

"Many Americans don't like the simple things. That's
what they have against we conservatives."

> —BARRY GOLDWATER, 1964

"Communism is twentieth-century Americanism."

> —Slogan of the American Communist Party, 1930s and
> 1940s

"We are not intervening in the internal affairs of this
country. . . ."

> —Secretary of State JOHN FOSTER DULLES, testifying about
> the 1957 CIA-supported revolt against Indonesian Presi-
> dent Sukarno, March 1958

"The world is divided into two groups of people: the
Christian anti-Communists, and the others."

> —Attributed to JOHN FOSTER DULLES

"Like good Christians."

> —WARREN AUSTIN, U.S. ambassador to the United Na-
> tions during the 1948 Mideast war, on how he hoped the
> Jews and Arabs would settle their differences

"While I cannot take the time to name all of the men in
the State Department who have been named as members
of the Communist Party and members of a spy ring, I
have here in my hand a list of 205 that were known to the
Secretary of State as being members of the Communist
Party and who nevertheless are still working and shaping
the policy of the State Department."

> —Senator JOSEPH R. McCARTHY, February 9, 1950,
> Wheeling, West Virginia, inaugurating his "witch-hunt"
> for Communists in government. Actually, McCarthy
> never "named" more than a few of the alleged 205 on his
> "list."

"I think this is the most unheard-of-thing I ever heard of."
> —Senator JOSEPH R. McCARTHY, on a ruling of the chairman of the Senate select committee charging him with conduct unbecoming a member of the Senate, August 26, 1954

"McCarthy did not intend the statement to be accepted at face value."
> —ROY COHN, 1968, on the Senator's famous charge that the Democratic party was guilty of twenty years of treason

"You hear about 'constitutional rights,' 'free speech' and the 'free press.' Every time I hear these words I say to myself, 'That man is a Red!! . . .' You never hear a *real* American talk like that!"
> —Mayor FRANK HAGUE of Jersey City

"The first duty of a revolutionary is to get away with it."
> —ABBIE HOFFMAN

"I think the credibility gap will rapidly disappear. It is events that cause the credibility gap, not the fact that a President deliberately lies or misleads the people. That is my opinion."
> —RICHARD NIXON

"I am opposed to the antilynching bill because the federal government has no more business enacting a law against one kind of murder than another. I am against the FEPC [Fair Employment Practices Commission] because if a man can tell you whom you must hire, he can tell you whom you cannot employ. I have met this head on."
> —LYNDON JOHNSON, while running for the U.S. Senate from Texas, 1948. Later he became a civil rights advocate, sponsoring the Civil Rights Act of 1964.

"I sleep each night a little better, and a little more confidently, because Lyndon Johnson is my President."
 —JACK VALENTI, presidential aide, 1965

"I resent the insinuendos."
 —Mayor RICHARD DALEY of Chicago

"God loves Richard Nixon."

    —THE REVEREND SUN MYUNG MOON

"Your commitment and compassion, your humanitarian principles and your interest in protecting individual liberty and freedom have made an outstanding contribution to furthering the cause of human dignity."

    —Secretary of Health, Education and Welfare JOSEPH CA-
    LIFANO, in a letter to the Reverend Jim Jones in Guyana,
    as reported in the *New Republic,* December 2, 1978. After
    the Jonestown massacre, Califano could not recall any
    such letter.

"Chris, they're trying to get me for something that has been going on ever since this country was founded."

—Spiro Agnew, complaining of the charges against him to Christian Dahl, his Democratic predecessor as executive of Baltimore County

"I will not resign if indicted. Our Constitution says that every man is entitled to a fair trial and a presumption of innocence. I intend to rely on the spirit as well as the letter of the guarantee. I would forsake the principles of the Founding Fathers if I abandoned this fight. And I do not intend to abandon it. . . ."

—Spiro Agnew, a few days before he resigned the vice-presidency on October 10, 1973

"There is a mysticism about men. There is quiet confidence. You look a man in the eye and you know he's got it—brains. This guy has got it. If he doesn't, Nixon has made a bum choice."

—Richard Nixon, at a press party after the 1968 Republican Convention in which he chose Agnew as his running mate

"Perhaps if we could talk only to the American people, we could tell a lot of secrets, but there is no way you can talk to the American people. Other people listen in."

—William B. Macomber, Jr., deputy under secretary of state and an ex-CIA official, on why the material in the Pentagon Papers could not have been released to the public

"It depends on who you're talking to. If you're talking to the head of the KGB and you happen to be overheard, and you're Jane Fonda or somebody else, there's no reason you shouldn't be overheard if somebody has the capability to overhear you—which I don't know if they do or not."

—Nelson Rockefeller, on electronic surveillance conducted by the National Security Agency

"My wife is delighted to get away . . . and it's fun for the kids."

> —JAMES R. SCHLESINGER, chairman of the Atomic Energy Commission, on why he took his family to watch the five-megaton nuclear explosion on Amchitka Island, 1972

"The tougher things get, the cooler I get."

> —RICHARD NIXON, according to Russell Baker

". . . some Nervous Nellies and some who will become frustrated and bothered and break ranks under the strain. And some will turn on their own leaders and their own country, and on our fighting men."

> —LYNDON JOHNSON, attacking critics of the Vietnam War, May 17, 1966

"I could be the most famous Jewish outlaw next to the Maccabees."

> —ABBIE HOFFMAN

"If you were on a plane and the pilot was drunk, you could tell, but if he was on marijuana, you couldn't."

> —RONALD REAGAN, arguing against pot

"Suppose I went in and told the President I was resigning. He could have a heart attack and you'd have Spiro Agnew as President. Do you want that? No? So don't keep telling me to resign."

> —HENRY KISSINGER, reportedly, to liberals who told him they would no longer serve as his advisers after the invasion of Cambodia. They suggested that he resign, May 8, 1970.

"I may have a lack of imagination, but I fail to see the moral issue involved."

> —HENRY KISSINGER, asked about his role in the Cambodian war, in which an estimated 500,000 people died

"A revolt of Guatemalans against Guatemalans."
>—HENRY CABOT LODGE, U.S. ambassador to the United Nations, on the CIA-financed, -organized, and -run coup in Guatemala against the leftist regime of Jacobo Arbenz Guzmán, 1954

"At one time we had a two-dollar poll tax in about six or eight states in the South. We don't believe in ignoramuses and illiterates voting. They don't know how to vote. They can be driven to the polls just like sheep. That's why we've got so many nuts in Washington."
>—Governor ROSS BARNETT of Mississippi, in the early 1960s

"If Lincoln were alive today, he'd roll over in his grave."
>—GERALD FORD

"Don't confuse me with the facts. I've got a closed mind."
>—Congressman EARL LANDGREBE of Indiana, a committed Nixon supporter, confronted with the "smoking gun" evidence of the Watergate recordings, 1979

"I don't think there is any reason to believe there would have been one dollar more for domestic programs had there been no Vietnam War."
>—JOSEPH A. CALIFANO, Secretary of Health, Education and Welfare and one of the chief architects of the "Great Society" programs

"I have said this before, but I shall say it again and again and again: Your boys are not going to be sent into any foreign wars."
>—FRANKLIN D. ROOSEVELT, campaign pledge, October 1940

"We are not about to send American boys nine or ten thousand miles away from home to do what Asian boys ought to be doing for themselves."
>—LYNDON JOHNSON, campaign pledge, October 1964

"We could pave the whole country and put parking stripes on it and still be home by Christmas."
—RONALD REAGAN, on Vietnam

"The Churchill of Asia."
—LYNDON JOHNSON, on Ngo Dinh Diem, president of South Vietnam, May 1961

"Now, the overthrow . . . of the Diem regime was a purely Vietnamese affair. We never participated in the planning. We never gave any advice. We had nothing whatever to do with it."
—HENRY CABOT LODGE, U.S. ambassador to Vietnam, on the U.S.-supported and -encouraged coup against Diem, June 30, 1964

"The People's Temple [Jim Jones] is a powerful force for change in the United States. . . ."
—MARK LANE, Jones's attorney

"Someday this will make a great opera, and I'd sure like the rights to it."
—San Francisco city supervisor HARVEY MILK, commenting on the tragedy in Guyana, shortly before he himself was killed, 1978

"A Saint."
—ANDREW YOUNG on Ayatollah Ruhollah Khomeini

"If it takes a bloodbath, let's get it over with. No more appeasement."
—RONALD REAGAN, on dealing with campus radicals, 1970

"Any student at any university in the United States who has an idea on how to bridge the gap between students and government should write it down and send it to the White House."
—TRICIA NIXON

"My goal is at the age of thirty-five to act like I'm fifteen."
>—JERRY RUBIN, radical, 1968

"The first part of the Yippie program, you know, is kill your parents. And I mean that quite seriously. Because until you're prepared to kill your parents, you're not really prepared to change the country because our parents are our first oppressors."
>—JERRY RUBIN, at Kent State University, 1970

"Well, I think you have to rebel against your parents to discover your identity, and then you have to love your parents to love yourself because you are your parents."
>—JERRY RUBIN, after analysis, on *The Dick Cavett Show*, April 1974

"I know that I can be more effective today working on Wall Street. . . . Money and financial interest will capture the passion of the eighties."
>—JERRY RUBIN, stockbroker, August 1980

"Money is power."
>—JERRY RUBIN, entrepreneur . . . impresario of the Jerry Rubin Business Networking Salon, 1982

"I'm confident . . . truth will become the hallmark of the Nixon administration. . . . We feel that we will be able to eliminate any possibility of a credibility gap in this administration."
>—HERBERT G. KLEIN, after being appointed communications director for the executive branch, November 25, 1968

"We are ending the war . . . the war is trending down, and I assure you it will continue to trend down."
>—HENRY KISSINGER, in a private meeting with Daniel Ellsberg, 1971. The morning after this statement was made the preinvasion bombing of Laos began.

"It's like football. You run a play and it fails. Then you turn around and call the same play again because they aren't expecting it."
>—RICHARD NIXON, on military action in Vietnam

"Peace with honor."
>—RICHARD NIXON, on the peace he would achieve in Vietnam, June 4, 1973

"Franklin D. Roosevelt is no crusader. He is no tribune of the people. He is no enemy of entrenched privilege. He is a pleasant man who, without any important qualifications for the office, would very much like to be President."
>—WALTER LIPPMANN, political analyst, 1932

"Don't bring up that damnable subject of politics in which I have no damned interest."
>—DWIGHT D. EISENHOWER, 1944

"Look, son, I cannot conceive of any circumstances that could draw out of me permission to consider me for any political post from dogcatcher to Grand High Supreme King of the Universe."
>—DWIGHT D. EISENHOWER, at a Pentagon press conference, 1948

"I am not available for and could not accept nomination for high public office. My decision is definite and positive."
>—DWIGHT D. EISENHOWER, 1948

"I am an actor and I intend to keep on acting."
>—RONALD REAGAN, in answer to a question from Sheilah Graham on whether he intended to run for governor of California, 1965

"Anyone who suggests I run for governor is no friend of mine. It's a terrible position, and besides, it requires living in Albany, which is small-town life at its worst. I wouldn't even consider it."

> —New York mayor ED KOCH in an interview with *Playboy*, April 1982. A few months later, he accepted the gubernatorial bid.

"My prime motive in going to the White House is to bring America back to God."

> —WARREN G. HARDING, whose administration ended in a blaze of revelations about official corruption

"I'm not asking for popularity; I'm not seeking it. In fact, if you really want to know, I care nothing for popularity. I can afford to say what I think. I am referring to what is genuine in me. Take actors, for instance; the really good ones don't rely on mere technique. They also follow their feelings when they play a part. Like me, they are genuine."

> —HENRY KISSINGER, in an interview with Oriana Fallaci

"If you think the United States has stood still, who built the largest shopping center in the world?"

> —RICHARD NIXON

"If we have to start over again with another Adam and Eve, then I want them to be Americans and not Russians, and I want them to be on this continent and not in Europe."

> —Senator RICHARD B. RUSSELL, supporting the antiballistic-missile system, 1969

"The ability to get to the verge without getting into the war is the necessary art. If you cannot master it, you inevitably get into war. If you try to run away from it, if you are scared to go to the brink, you are lost."

> —Secretary of State JOHN FOSTER DULLES, on "brinkmanship," 1956

"Mr. Nixon was the thirty-seventh President of the United States. He has been preceded by thirty-six others."
—GERALD FORD, 1974

"Democracy will be dead by 1950."
—JOHN LANGDON-DAVIES, *A Short History of the Future* (1936)

"Admiration flows abundantly from/this pen of mine/For the man who's giving all he's got/To try and save mankind."
—LUCI BAINES JOHNSON, verse to her father, 1965

"The happiest President the country ever had."
—JULIE NIXON EISENHOWER, describing her father during a TV interview, 1969

"It's amazing what he has done to the media . . . helping it to reform itself."
—TRICIA NIXON COX, in admiration for Spiro Agnew

"The race will not be close at all. Landon will be overwhelmingly elected and I'll stake my reputation as a prophet on it."
—WILLIAM RANDOLPH HEARST, commenting on the presidential contest between Franklin Delano Roosevelt and Alf Landon, August 1936

"I surveyed the closely knit group around Tom Dewey who will take over the White House eighty-six days from now."
—DREW PEARSON, in his column the day before the election of Harry S Truman, 1948

"Ninety percent accurate 40 percent of the time."
—DREW PEARSON, on his political predictions

"In every country the Communists have taken over, the first thing they do is outlaw cockfighting."
> —Oklahoma state representative JOHN MONKS, speaking in opposition to a bill to outlaw the sport in his state, 1975

"I am firmly against the kind of logrolling which would subject our defense program to narrowly sectional or selfish pulling or hauling ... [but] I am getting pretty hot under the collar about the way my state of West Virginia is shortchanged by the Army, Navy, and Air Force."
> —Congressman KENNETH HECHLER of West Virginia

"I guess we concentrated too much on Pike County."
> —Ohio gubernatorial candidate FRAZIER REAMS, after learning he captured only Pike out of the state's eighty-eight counties

"Never trust anyone over thirty."
> —JACK WEINBERG, University of California student—according to *Playboy* (April 1970), the originator of this phrase

"We love your adherence to Democratic principles. . . ."
> —Vice-President GEORGE BUSH to Philippine president Ferdinand Marcos, whose regime has been much criticized for its repressive measures, September 1982

"My life's an ad for the revolution."
> —ABBIE HOFFMAN

"There is no place in our campaign or in the electoral process for this type of activity, and we will not permit or condone it."
> —JOHN MITCHELL, in his first statement after the news of the Watergate burglary broke, June 18, 1972

"It's nice to be back in Alabama."
> —JOHN MITCHELL, on entering prison at Maxwell Air Force Base, 1977

"I am not a crook."
> —RICHARD NIXON, November 1973

"When the President does it, that means it is not illegal."
> —RICHARD NIXON, in a TV interview with David Frost, May 20, 1977

"I believe President Nixon—like Abraham Lincoln—is a man uniquely suited to serve our nation in time of crisis."
> —GERALD FORD

"I cast light on the issues; my opponent plunges them into darkness."
> —Senator JOHN TOWER of Texas, during his 1978 re-election campaign

"This so-called war is nothing but about twenty-five people and propaganda."
> —Senator ARTHUR VANDENBERG of Michigan, a month after the German invasion of Poland, 1939

"A spirit of national masochism prevails, encouraged by an effete corps of impudent snobs who characterize themselves as intellectuals."
> —SPIRO AGNEW, October 4, 1969

"In short, Agnew wouldn't sound like Agnew if he were President—and, in a sense, properly so."
> —WILLIAM F. BUCKLEY, in a *Playboy* interview, May 1970

"Sputnik doesn't worry me one iota. Apparently from what they say, they have put one small ball in the air."
> —DWIGHT D. EISENHOWER, 1957

"Now I answer questions, but I only answer the questions that are asked."

> —Secretary of Defense MELVIN LAIRD, on why he had not mentioned the air attack on Son Tay near Hanoi (November 1970) when testifying before the Senate Foreign Relations Committee. The United States had denied the raid, claiming to have bombed only south of the 19th parallel.

"They have vilified me, they have crucified me, yes, they have even criticized me."

> —Mayor RICHARD DALEY of Chicago

"The streets are safe in Philadelphia; it's only the people who make them unsafe."

> —Mayor FRANK RIZZO of Philadelphia

"I would remind you that extremism in defense of liberty is no vice and . . . moderation in the pursuit of justice is no virtue."

> —BARRY GOLDWATER, 1964

"It's inherent in [the] government's right, if necessary, to lie to save itself when it's going up into a nuclear war. That seems to me basic—basic."

> —ARTHUR SYLVESTER, assistant secretary of defense for public affairs, about the "cold" President Kennedy had reportedly suffered during the missile crisis, December 6, 1962

"Sin began with Adam. If you turn the lights out, folks will steal. They'll do that in Switzerland, too."

> —ANDREW YOUNG, on the looting during the power blackout in New York City

Martha Mitchell: "Name one woman who was persecuted more, just name one."

Reporter: "How about Joan of Arc?"

Martha Mitchell: "She only burned."

"As a matter of fact, Nancy never had any interest in politics or anything else when we got married."
—RONALD REAGAN

"This population is too hopelessly split up into races and factions to govern it under universal suffrage, except by the bribery of patronage and corruption."
—WILLIAM "BOSS" TWEED of Tammany Hall, justifying his school of political management

"The Cold War is a good war. It is the only war in history where the question of destruction doesn't enter into it at all."
—PAUL HOFFMAN, head of the Economic Cooperation Administration (1948–50), the agency that administered the Marshall Plan

"Resources are there to be used. I don't believe in hoarding resources for the sake of hoarding."
—Secretary of Agriculture EARL T. BUTZ, on his anticonservationist stand, 1976

"What America needs is a sense of humor."
—LARRY VAN HOOSE, executive director of the Republican party in Kentucky, defending Earl Butz's headline-making recitation of a racial joke, October 4, 1976

"We're just a simple apostolic society, that anybody with a sensitive eye and ear couldn't help but appreciate."
—THE REVEREND JIM JONES, of his cult

"I want to say this to you whites in the audience, and whites everywhere, that if you think there were riots after Martin Luther King was killed, this nation won't survive if anything happens to Adam Clayton Powell."
—ADAM CLAYTON POWELL, 1968

"You've got to forget about this civilian. Whenever you drop bombs, you're going to hit civilians."
—BARRY GOLDWATER, January 23, 1967

"My great-great-grandfather died at the Alamo."
—LYNDON JOHNSON, winding up a stirring address to Vietnam-bound servicemen in Seoul, 1966. The President, as he later explained, "got his tongue twisted in the emotion of the moment"—none of his forebears was at the Alamo.

"The fact that my father was President and Chief Justice of the United States was a tremendous help and inspiration in my public career."
—ROBERT A. TAFT

"If Kennedy runs in '80, I'll whip his ass."
—JIMMY CARTER, 1979

"I always felt the White House would stand behind me."
—EDWARD KENNEDY, 1979

"When one persuades or conquers someone, one mustn't deceive them."
—HENRY KISSINGER, December 1972

Nixon: "Do you want to go this route now? Let it hang out, so to speak?"

Dean: "Well, it isn't really that ..."

Haldeman: "It's a limited hang-out."

Dean: "It is a limited hang-out. It's not an absolute hang-out."
—*The Presidential Transcripts*

"When information which properly belongs to the public is systematically withheld by those in power, the people soon become ignorant of their own affairs, distrustful of those who manage them, and—eventually—incapable of determining their own destinies."
>—RICHARD NIXON, March 8, 1972

"They should get off Nixon's back and let him be President, because he's a damn good one. He's also got a great-looking nose."
>—BOB HOPE, commenting on Watergate, in a *Playboy* interview, December 1973

"He is our President, and I feel that if Richard Nixon is impeached, there will be mass suicides, mass nervous breakdowns, and total demoralization of the country."
>—MRS. HELEN BUFFINGTON, branch vice-chairperson, Committee to Reelect the President

"A vote against MX production today is a vote against arms control tomorrow."
>—RONALD REAGAN, December 1982

FOREIGN AFFAIRS

"Had I been present at the creation, I would have given some useful hints for the better ordering of the universe."
—ALFONSO THE WISE (1221–1284)

"I am the King of Rome, and above grammar."
—SIGISMUND (1368–1437), at the Council of Constance

"What God hath joined together, let no man put asunder."
—HENRY VIII, in a book sent to Pope Leo on the subject of marriage; this was, of course, *before* the monarch decided to divorce Catherine of Aragon, the first of his eight wives.

"I know I am doing my duty and therefore can never wish to retract."
—GEORGE III, refusing to abandon his disastrous course in regard to the American colonies

"I see no point in reading."
—LOUIS XIV

"They accuse Rasputin of kissing women, etc. Read the Apostles; they kissed everybody as a form of greeting."
—TSARINA ALEXANDRA of Russia, excusing her favorite, the erratic priest Rasputin, who had been accused of seducing, kissing, and raping indiscriminately

"Executions are so much a part of British history that it is almost impossible for many excellent people to think of the future without them."
—VISCOUNT TEMPLEWOOD, *In the Shadow of the Gallows* (1951)

"When I want a peerage, I shall buy one like an honest man."
—Attributed to LORD NORTHCLIFFE

"The Aga Khan is held by his followers to be the direct descendant of God. An English Duke takes precedence."
—Heralds of the College of Arms, quoted in *Reader's Digest,* March 1958

"This sort of thing may be tolerated by the French, but we are British—thank God."
—VISCOUNT MONTGOMERY, on the Homosexuality Bill, May 1965

"Mussolini is always right."
—Italian Fascist slogan

"On my grave I want this epigraph: 'Here lies one of the most intelligent animals ever to appear on the surface of the earth!' "
—BENITO MUSSOLINI, December 1937

"Germany neither intends nor wishes to interfere in the internal affairs of Austria, to annex Austria, or to conclude an *Anschluss.*"

> —ADOLF HITLER, May 21, 1935; in March, 1938, the *Anschluss* took place and Austria was occupied by German troops.

"Germany has no desire to attack Czechoslovakia."

> —ADOLF HITLER, May 7, 1936; in 1939 Germany annexed parts of that nation.

"The Sudetenland is the last territorial claim which I have to make in Europe."

> —ADOLF HITLER, September 26, 1938

"Germany and Poland are two nations, and these nations will live, and neither of them will be able to do away with the other."

> —ADOLF HITLER, May 1, 1938; Hitler's invasion of Poland in September 1939 marked the beginning of World War II.

"Only warmongers think there will be war. I think there will be a long period of peace."

> —ADOLF HITLER, January 30, 1939

"This is the second time in our history that there has come back from Germany to Downing Street Peace with Honour: I believe it is peace for our time."

> —Prime Minister NEVILLE CHAMBERLAIN, returning from the Munich Conference, September 30, 1938

"After all, they are only going into their own back garden."

> —LORD LOTHIAN, commenting on Hitler's military occupation of the Rhineland, 1936

"Let's be friends."

> —ADOLF HITLER to French correspondent Bertrand de Jouvenel, March 1936

"I never thought Hitler was such a bad chap. ..."

> —THE DUKE OF WINDSOR to Lord Kinross, twenty years after World War II

"By compelling Germany to sign a non-aggression pact, the Soviet Union tremendously limited the direction of Nazi war aims."

> —*The Daily Worker* on the Soviet-German pact, August 1939; one week later, Hitler invaded Poland.

"We have always stood and we stand today for the non-interference in the internal affairs of other countries. We have always abided, and we shall abide, by these positions."

> —NIKITA KHRUSHCHEV, in an article in *Foreign Affairs*, October 1959

"The countries of Eastern Europe have already been liberated."

> —NIKITA KHRUSHCHEV, in answer to a question as to whether a "war of liberation" could take place in Europe as well as in the Third World

"Nobody intends to put up a wall."

> —WALTER ULBRICHT, East German Communist party boss, at a press conference in East Berlin, June 16, 1961. On August 13, 1961, the Berlin Wall was erected.

"According to information received from Cape Canaveral, the rocket with a man on board was launched. After fifteen minutes the capsule with the pilot, Alan Shepard, fell in the Atlantic Ocean."

> —Soviet news release about the first manned space flight— which was totally successful

"Gaiety is the most outstanding feature of the Soviet Union."
> —Joseph Stalin, 1935

"It's useful to have been somewhere."
> —Prime Minister Joe Clark of Canada, asked why he had embarked on a foreign tour, 1979

"The Olympic Games can no more have a deficit than a man can have a baby."
> —Mayor Jean Drapeau of Montreal, just before the financially disastrous Montreal Olympic Games of 1976

"If the cabbage is too expensive for you, buy something else."
> —Finance Minister Jean Chrétien of Canada, on soaring food prices, 1979

"If I had not been born Perón, I would have liked to be Perón."

—JUAN PERÓN

"My simple woman's heart . . ."

—EVA PERÓN

"Baader had the perfidy to shoot himself in the back of his head to try to make us look like murderers."

—West German Interior Minister WERNER MAIHOFER, on the death of terrorist Andreas Baader, 1977

"I consider myself to be the most important figure in the world."

—President IDI AMIN of Uganda, August 11, 1976

"Your experience will be a lesson to all of us men to be careful not to marry ladies in a very high position."

> —IDI AMIN, in a message to Lord Snowden expressing regrets over the breakup of his marriage to Princess Margaret, 1976

"We are paying much more attention to human rights here than in many other countries. At least here we have security in our homes, and you won't get a knife in your stomach if you walk down the street."

> —MOHAMMED REZA PAHLAVI, shah of Iran, June 1978

"I think there should be a limit [to power] because men who exercise high responsibilities, especially in the starting of a revolution, have many opportunities to become vain—to become gods."

> —FIDEL CASTRO, 1977

"There is no personality cult in Cuba."

> —FIDEL CASTRO, 1977

"People make me out to be a very devilish person. Actually I'm just a simple farmer."

> —ANASTASIO SOMOZA, Nicaraguan dictator, 1978

"You can afford democracy because you are so rich. In the Philippines there was anarchy. We had to do something to stop it."

> —IMELDA MARCOS, first lady of the Philippines

"[Flogging] is not a matter of degradation of a human being, but a matter of deterrence."

> —President MOHAMMAD ZIA UL-HAQ of Pakistan, defending his country's practice of flogging criminals, December 1982

"Maybe prisoners were tortured in the old days, but that doesn't happen any longer."

—FARAH DIBA PAHLAVI, empress of Iran, 1977

"The ancient poets of China said, 'The flowers perfume the air, the moon shines, man has a long life.' Allow me to give a new explanation of these poetic terms. The flowers perfume the air—this means that the flowers of the art of socialist realism are incomparably beautiful. The moon shines—this means that the sputnik has opened a new era in the conquest of space. Man has a long life—this means that the great Soviet Union will live tens and thousands of years."

—MAO DUN, Red Chinese writer, in *Pravda*, May 1957

"If my leaps were as high as the thoughts of Chairman Mao, they would need a fireman's ladder to measure the crossbar."

—NI CHIH-CHIN, Red Chinese high jumper, after clearing an almost record-breaking jump at the Games of the New Emerging Forces in Cambodia, 1966

"What's wrong with taping a conversation when you happen to have a tape recorder with you? Most people in America love playing with tape recorders."

—MAO ZEDONG, on Richard Nixon

"We are not at war with Egypt. We are in an armed conflict."

—SIR ANTHONY EDEN, at the time of the Suez crisis, November 4, 1956

"We will never negotiate with them directly . . . we will not give up one inch of our territory and we will not negotiate with Israel under any circumstances. . . ."

—President ANWAR EL-SADAT of Egypt, April 25, 1972

"I have a right to express my belief that there is no one guilty in Israel."
>—Prime Minister MENACHEM BEGIN of Israel, September 26, 1982, on the massacre by Lebanese troops of Palestinians in Beirut refugee camps

"He uses the Arabic language, which is full of hyperbole, and when it is translated into English, it means completely other than what he says."
>—MOHAMMED T. MEHDI, president of the Arab-American Relations Association, explaining the statements of Libya's Colonel Muammar Qaddafi

"You know, I can't understand why anyone would want to join the opposition. There are so many opportunities in government. . . ."
>—EMIR ABBAS HOVEIDA, prime minister of Iran under the shah, 1974

"I'm persuaded that the monarchy in Iran will last longer than your regimes. Or maybe I ought to say that your regimes won't last and mine will."
>—MOHAMMED REZA PAHLAVI, shah of Iran, to Frances FitzGerald, 1974

"Nobody can overthrow me—I have the power."
>—MOHAMMED REZA PAHLAVI, shah of Iran, 1978

"I would very much like to take a vacation."
>—MOHAMMED REZA PAHLAVI, shah of Iran, 1979

"It is unjust and unhuman to call me a dictator."
>—AYATOLLAH RUHOLLAH KHOMEINI to Oriana Fallaci, October 1979

"They will be hit on the head with iron bars or the sword until they are reformed."
>—AYATOLLAH RUHOLLAH KHOMEINI, 1981

"We cannot afford to have such an ambiguous concept placed in our Constitution."
>   —AYATOLLAH KHOMEINI, on why he refused to have the word "democratic" in the constitution of the Islamic Republic

"We would hate to impose another [oil] embargo."
>   —PRINCE FAHD, Saudi Arabia's minister of the interior, 1975

"Do you know how much we pay for a barrel of mineral water? Double what you pay for a barrel of excellent crude oil. Our attitude therefore seems justified to me."
>   —SHEIKH AHMAD ZAKI YAMANI of Saudi Arabia, 1975

"The politics of the world is too serious a business to be left any more to foreigners."
>   —*Spectator* c. 1970

ADS

"Some things you decide with your heart. The things that matter. Like your stainless."
> —Ad in *Bride's Magazine* for Oneida stainless steel

"NOW YOU CAN ENJOY DYING. Call today for information about clean, dry, ventilated entombment at special preconstruction prices."
> —Ad for Rosewood Memorial Park in Tidewater, West Virginia

"Not a cough in a carload."
> —Ad for Old Gold cigarettes, 1940s

"Reach for a Lucky instead of a sweet."
> —Ad for Lucky Strike cigarettes, 1930s

"So safe, so pure, it's used to filter the air in leading hospitals."
> —Ad for Kent's Micronite-filter cigarettes, 1953

"Just what the doctor ordered."
> —Ad for L&M cigarettes with "Pure White Miracle Tip of Alpha-Cellulose," mid-1950s

"Basically, the image we want for cigarettes is that they are used by a fun-loving, active group."
> —DAVID LADD, advertising director of P. Lorillard Co., 1962

"If you're not helping to save hunting, you are helping to outlaw it."
> —Ad against gun control

"Completely non-poisonous . . . safe . . . astonishingly safe . . . non-toxic . . . fully harmless. . . ."
> —Advertising by Grünenthal Chemical Co. when thalidomide was first launched on the market, 1957

"This place is the preferred resort for those wanting solitude. People searching for such solitude are in fact flock-
ing here from all corners of the globe."
　　—Prospectus for a Swiss resort

"Mexico! The amigo country! Where the excitement
hasn't lessened . . . the beauty hasn't diminished . . . and
the fun hasn't stopped in over two thousand years!"
　　—Tag line to a television spot by the Mexican Tourist
　　Council

"Keep an eye on your wife! Possibly she's not as happy as
she seems. Sometimes you may catch her when she's off
guard and surprise a little wistful look on her face. Is she
worrying about you? After all, most wives are loyal and
proud, and rather reluctant to speak up. . . . There is a
chance she's distressed because you aren't as careful about
shaving as you were in times past. . . ."
　　—Gillette ad, 1930

"The smart car for the younger executive or the professional family on the way up."
　　—David Wallace, manager of the Edsel marketing-research
　　department of Ford, describing the advertising image for
　　the highly promoted car that was to prove a major disas-
　　ter in the marketplace, 1957

"Drowsy with love and smoldering with desire, her
haunting eyes ruled gay Vienna and caused brave hearts
to beat faster beneath tight tunics."
　　—Advertising for Mae Murray in *The Merry Widow,* 1920s

"Her magnetism is the divine logic of art, as potent as the perfume of the tuberose which sways the senses. People who saw her first picture *Passion* left the theater feeling that they had experienced an electric storm."
> —Paramount Pictures on its leading femme fatale, Theda Bara, 1925

"Love means never having to say you're sorry."
> —Tag line for Erich Segal's *Love Story* (1970)

"Melina [the star] is irresistible."
> —Abridged quote from critic Edwin Newman in a *New York Times* ad for the Broadway musical *Ilya Darling* (1967). What Newman had actually said was *"Ilya Darling* rests on the premise that Melina Mercouri is irresistible. Even if one accepts this unlikely premise, this is a tasteless, heavy-handed show beyond anyone's capacity to bring to life." When the full statement came out, the advertiser described the ad as a "regrettable error caused by the heat of an advertising deadline. . . ."

"Detect Earthquakes!! At home in your spare time. Glamorous life of an Earthquake Sentry yours for only $5. Includes seismotron, 2-ft. cord, earthquake comic. Earthquake striking your town? Be the first to know! Whole community will beg you for tips!"
> —Ad placed by the California Earthquake Institute, Fresno, California

"His heart quickened at the soft fragrance of her cheeks, BUT HER SHOES HID A SORRY CASE OF ATHLETE'S FOOT."
> —Ad, 1930s

"Reading is to the mind what Calvin's are to the body."
> —BROOKE SHIELDS, in a series of TV spot ads for Calvin Klein jeans, September 1980

"What would New York be without the Diors?—Newark."

> —Planned slogan for a Dior advertising campaign, before it aroused community ire in Newark, 1982. Withdrawing the offending line, the president of Christian Dior, New York, commented to the Newark City Council: "It was not the intention of the company to slander any individual or city. I was not aware of all the terrific things going on in Newark."

"Pajamas are a cloak for a man and his dreams. They are retreat, sanctuary, shelter. Pajamas are tranquillity, a gateway to privacy. They are illusionary, for pleasures unguessable."

> —Ad for Excello pajamas, 1961

"Evans-Piconery! Is to wonderful in. Whimsy in. Very appeal to him in. These sweater wonderfuls."

> —Ad for Evans-Picone sweaters

"Be with Jesus every minute of the day. Wear the watch on your hand of the man who stilled the water, complete with ever-revolving crimson heart and our Savior's likeness beautifully reproduced in six colors—in the race of your choice."

> —Ad in a rock newspaper for a watch for Jesus freaks, 1971

"[Royal Bee Formula Capsules] can bring 'the Joy of Life' back into aging bodies . . . solve nagging 'Change of Life' problems in men and women . . . produce a state of buoyant well-being."

> —Ad for Royal Bee Formula Capsules, a "health" product

"Afraid of A-Bomb contamination? In the event of an A-Bomb attack wash contamination away with Flobar. . . . It can be carried about for immediate use."

> —Ad for Flobar, early 1950s

"Buy furs wisely . . . and you can save to buy War Bonds."
—Fur ad, 1940s

"Communist Jewish purge now places the seal upon Nazi partnership. Mass murders, suppression of religious and human rights, are unknown facts of these kindred brotherhoods. Could it happen to us? Not while we have family life and the influence of the traditional open fire which draws so many together in the modern, mellow warmth circle around so many trouble-free Fireplaces which radiate that sleepy, soothing, satisfying mellow warmth when made and fixed by Longhard and Braithwaite, Ltd."
—Ad for a fireplace-equipment company in the *Bolton* (England) *Evening News,* 1953

"Drink Schlitz in Brown Bottles and Avoid That Skunk Taste."
—Old billboard sign for Schlitz, recalled by Ernest Hemingway

"Breathtakingly beautiful."
—Ad for a new kind of hearse in *Casket and Sunnyside,* 1950s

"I begin to see that it's advertising that makes America hum. It gives ginks like me a goal. Makes us want something. And the world is so much better for our heaving a little harder. Looking at the advertisements makes me think I've GOT to succeed. Every advertisement is an advertisement for success. I guess one reason there is so much success in America is because there is so much advertising—of things to want—things to work for."
—"Andy Consumer," explaining the value of advertising in a full-page ad in *Life,* 1925

SPORTS

"I am the best. I just haven't played yet."
>—MUHAMMAD ALI (Cassius Clay), asked if he played golf, 1966

"Arnold is the greatest putter in the world. He's better than I am—and I'm the best."
>—LEE TREVINO, winner of the U.S. Open, on why he planned to sponsor Dallas amateur Arnold Salinas on the pro tour, 1968

"Everybody knows I'm the best, so why bother to play?"
>—BOBBY FISCHER, before his chess match with Boris Spassky in Iceland, 1972

"I'm the best heavyweight fighter in Canada and I'll be the best until I'm dead seven years."
>—GEORGE CHUVALO, stripped of his Canadian heavyweight championship which he had held for twenty-one years, 1979

"My greatest strength is that I have no weaknesses."
> —JOHN McENROE, tennis champion

"I thought the school had a commitment to soccer, but that wasn't the case. . . . Its emphasis was on academics."
> —KARL KREMSER, former place kicker for the Miami Dolphins, on why he stopped coaching soccer at Davidson College, 1980

"Winning isn't everything. It's the only thing."
> —VINCE LOMBARDI

"A team that won't be beaten, can't be beaten."
> —BILL ROPER, college football coach

"I hope I never see another fight for the rest of my life, believe me."
> —BILLY MARTIN, on taking over as manager of the Oakland A's, 1980

"I believe if God had ever managed, He would have been very aggressive, the way I manage."
> —BILLY MARTIN, 1981

"You know that no man can possibly talk like me who wasn't an educated man with a high degree of intelligence."
> —HOWARD COSELL

"Howard Cosell is one of the most intelligent men in the world today."
> —JOE THEISMAN, Washington Redskin quarterback, 1980

"I only wish to God I'd been on the Watergate committee. I think the questioning would have been a little bit stronger and more pertinent, very candidly."
> —HOWARD COSELL

"Ninety percent of this game is half mental."

> —JIM WOHLFORD, Milwaukee Brewers outfielder, on the subject of baseball, 1977

"He's not fired. He's just not rehired."

> —MIKE SHAW, publicity director of the NBA Buffalo Braves, on the termination of the contract of coach Jack Ramey, 1976

"I hate to see you go. We couldn't have won three straight world titles without you. I love you, buddy, and believe me when I tell you that."

> —CHARLES O. FINLEY, owner of the Oakland A's, to Vida Blue on the day he sold him to the New York Yankees

"You're making too much at a young age. It isn't good for you."

> —M. DONALD GRANT, chairman of the board of the New York Mets, to Tom Seaver before trading him to the Cincinnati Reds

"A man isn't supposed to love another man. But I love Willie. He's the best ballplayer I ever saw and I love the son of a gun. Emotionally, it's terrible."

> —HORACE STONEHAM, owner of the San Francisco Giants, after trading Willie Mays to the New York Mets, 1972

"This is bad for team morale."

> —HARVEY MURPHY, basketball coach at the University of North Carolina at Charlotte, after six of his eleven players were declared academically ineligible, 1966

"I'm just trying to make a better man of Nettles."

> —GEORGE STEINBRENNER, of a contract dispute in which he forced Yankee third baseman Graig Nettles to back down, 1977

"George [Steinbrenner] is misunderstood. All he really wants is a father-son relationship."

> —TOMMY JOHN, Yankee pitcher

"I've taken this team as far as I can."

> —LYNN WHEELER, coach of Iowa State's women's basketball team, resigning after it finished the season with fourteen straight defeats, 1980

"I got a message from beyond. I'm not well enough to fight."

> —CLEVELAND WILLIAMS, Tampa heavyweight, on why he refused to fight a scheduled match in Wales despite the certification of four doctors that he was in good health, 1958

"I coulda busted Joe Louis up real good if my manager woulda let me go out there and hit him all over. You know what I mean, hit him all over and explain later. Butt him and kick him around and do anything you can do. It's a fight, isn't it?"

> —"TWO-TON" TONY GALENTO, reminiscing, 1964

"I overslept."

> —CLAUDELL WILLIAMS, explaining why it took him four days to appear for baseball practice after being traded to the Chicago White Sox by the Texas Rangers, 1978

"I don't like the sight of blood. That's why I didn't get up."

> —JIM WINFIELD, boxer, explaining why he took the count kneeling on one knee, after being knocked out in fifty-five seconds of the first round by Bobo Renfrow, 1973

"We have only one person to blame, and that's each other."

> —BARRY BECK, New York Ranger defense, discussing a brawl at the Stanley Cup play-off game against the Los Angeles Kings, April 1981

"Anyone who will tear down sports will tear down America. Sports and religion have made America what it is today."
—WOODY HAYES

"Any ballplayer that don't sign autographs for little kids ain't American. He's a Communist."
—ROGERS HORNSBY, seven-time National League batting champion

"Critics of college football are kooks, crumbums and commies, hairy loud-mouth beatniks. Football is war—without killing. They are the custodians of the concepts of democracy. As football players, they possess a clear, bright, fighting spirit which is America itself!"
—MAX RAFFERTY, former California state superintendent of public instruction

"Athletics are the natural expression of the educated minds of he-men."
—SAMUEL J. FRATTO, candidate for governor of Wyoming, running on a platform that emphasized sports, 1958

"We want you to dress well, conduct yourselves well. We're not interested in youth rebellion or the campus oddballs you see here or elsewhere. People like that have what doctors call a psychosis to be noticed."
—PAUL BROWN, coach and general manager of the Cincinnati Bengals, 1969

"I have a conscience and I feel guilty if I don't do great things every day."
—JOE NAMATH

"Well, they tell me it can't be done, but sometimes it doesn't always work."
—CASEY STENGEL, after one of his plays for the Mets backfired

"We are all in this together, and don't you remember it."
> —BILL PETERSON, coach of the Houston Oilers, to his team

"I have nothing to say and I'm only going to say it once."
> —FRANK SMITH, coach of the Toronto Maple Leafs, 1979

"I feel good compassion between us."
> —GUS GANAKAS, Michigan State University basketball coach, after he suspended ten players but hoped to get them back on the squad

"It's about ninety percent strength and forty percent technique."
> —JOHNNY WALKER, world middleweight wrist-wrestling champion, 1980

"I wouldn't say that Joe has a sore arm per se, but his arm is kind of sore."
> —WEEB EWBANK, coach of the New York Jets, on why Joe Namath had missed a practice, 1969

"Even if I said [it] . . . I don't think I'd make a statement like that."
> —RAY GREBEY, chief negotiator for the owners during the 1981 baseball strike, questioned about one of his statements to the press

"I'd have played for nothing, but Paul insisted I take something."
> —STEVE CARLTON, pitching star of the Philadelphia Phillies, signed for $165,000 by General Manager Paul Owens, 1973

"I just want to play baseball."
> —REGGIE JACKSON, to Barbara Walters, on his lack of commercial interests

"A quarter of a million is peanuts."
> —BOBBY FISCHER, of the 1972 Reykjavik chess prize of $250,000

"I lost it in the sun!"

> —BILLY LOES, Brooklyn Dodger (1950–56), on why he was unable to catch a grounder in the 1952 World Series

"[Manager Bob Lemon] came out and said forget about the runners, so I forgot about them."

> —JIM BEATTIE, Yankee pitcher, who allowed the Milwaukee Braves to set up the tying run during a game, 1979

"I was picking up the players' caps. They cost $6.50 apiece."

> —TOM MURPHY, sixty-three-year-old assistant trainer for the Cincinnati Reds, asked what a man his age was doing in the middle of a brawl between the Reds and the Cardinals, 1967

"Well, that kind of puts the damper on even a Yankee win."

> —PHIL RIZZUTO, told of Pope Paul VI's death while broadcasting a Yankee game, 1978

"I read a book in college called 'Territorial Imperative.' A fellow always has to protect his master's home. . . . My territory is down and away from the hitters. If they're going out there and getting the ball, I'll have to come in close."

—BILL LEE, Boston Red Sox player (1969–76), justifying his use of the beanball

"That feller runs splendid but he needs help at the plate which coming from the country chasing rabbits all winter give him strong legs despite he broke one falling out of a tree which shows you can't tell and when a curveball comes he waves at it and if pitchers don't throw curves you have no pitching staff so how is a manager to know whether to tell boys to fall out of trees and break legs so he can run fast even if he can't hit a curveball?"

—CASEY STENGEL

"We need new blood in racing, but under present laws, by the time a boy or girl is twenty he or she may have taken up some other hobby."

> —JAMES DONN, JR., president of Gulfstream Park, recommending that the legal betting age be lowered from twenty-one to eighteen, 1963

"We're going to put those women right back where they belong like they used to be when we had the slippers and the pipe. . . . They were around the house and they didn't try to get out and get the man's job from him. They can't even do it half as good and they still want the same kind of money."

> —BOBBY RIGGS, a few weeks before his tennis defeat at the hands of Billie Jean King, 1973

"Sumo is a traditional sport, and we don't want to see a woman clad only in a Mawashi loincloth enter the ring before the public."

> —Directors of the Japan Sumo Association, explaining why they barred ten-year-old Mei Kurihara from the final round of a children's tournament after she had won an elimination round, 1978

"How did they get my picture? I've never been to New York."

> —SAM SNEAD, golfer, seeing his picture in a New York paper after his 1937 victory in the U.S. Open

"I don't know why people question the academic training of a student athlete. Half of the doctors in the country graduated in the bottom of their class."

> —AL MCGUIRE, basketball coach at Marquette University, 1976

"Sure they're better; they have different muscles."

> —ALVIN DARK, New York Giant, on the skills of black players, 1961

"It's okay for me to criticize my players because I sign the checks."

—GEORGE STEINBRENNER, 1981

"Good pitching always stops good hitting and vice versa."

—BOB VEALE, Pittsburgh Pirates pitcher, comparing the relative importance of pitching and hitting, 1966

"You have to treat death like any other part of life."

—TOM SNEVA, race-car driver, discussing the dangers of driving at Indy, 1977

"I think smoking is the thing I do good and most consistently. I hardly ever have an off day smoking. I smoke good and I smoke consistent. I can't think of anything else I am as consistently good at."

—DOUG RADER, Houston Astros third baseman, on his strengths and weaknesses

"When history records the great crossings, they will speak of Moses crossing the Red Sea, Caesar crossing the Rubicon, and Washington crossing the Delaware, but frankly, your crossing of the British channel must take its place alongside of these."

> —JIMMY WALKER, mayor of New York, to Gertrude Ederle on her swim across the English Channel, 1926

"I'm really not a wild guy. I always get to bed by two A.M. All that talk about six A.M. is crazy, man. I got to get my sleep."

> —BO BELINSKY, baseball player noted for his playboy predilections, 1963

"The trouble with officials is they just don't care who wins."

> —TOMMY CANTERBURY, Centenary College basketball coach, 1980

"Just a fad. A passing fancy."

> —PHIL WRIGLEY, baseball owner, on the future possibilities of night games

"It will probably be the greatest sports event in history. Bigger than the Frazier-Ali fight. It really is the free world against the lying, cheating, hypocritical Russians."

> —BOBBY FISCHER, on the world chess championship in Iceland, 1972

"I can't see anything wrong with good clean violence."

> —BOB TIMBERLAKE, Michigan quarterback, on why he saw no conflict between football and his ministerial ambitions, 1964

"Hurt is in your mind."

> —HARRY LOMBARDI, to his son, Vince

WOMEN

"I'm for women's lib, but I don't mind walking three paces behind Jerry."
—BETTY FORD

"All psychologists who have studied the intelligence of women . . . recognize today that they represent the most inferior forms of human evolution and that they are closer to children and savages than to an adult, civilized man. They excel in fickleness, inconstancy, absence of thought and logic, and incapacity to reason. Without doubt there exist some distinguished women, very superior to the average man, but they are as exceptional as the birth of any monstrosity, as, for example, of a gorilla with two heads; consequently, we may neglect them entirely."
—GUSTAVE LE BON, founder of social psychology, 1879

"Women are only children of a larger growth."
—LORD CHESTERFIELD

"All the pursuits of men are the pursuits of women also, but in all of them a woman is inferior to a man."
—PLATO

"Girls have an unfair advantage over men: if they can't get what they want by being smart, they can get it by being dumb."
—YUL BRYNNER, 1964

"I will not affirm that women have no character, rather they have a new one every day."
—HEINRICH HEINE

"I want women to have all the faults and weaknesses they always had. I adore them, but we must keep them in their place. It's presumptuous for a woman to show me she is a doctor of mathematics. Comptometers can do that. What's more subtle and difficult is to know how to make a man feel important."
—MARCELLO MASTROIANNI, 1965

"We women were designed to delight, excite and satisfy the male of the species."
—"J" (JOAN GARRITY), *The Sensuous Woman* (1969)

"A beautiful woman with a brain is like a beautiful woman with a clubfoot."
—BERNIE CORNFELD, entrepreneur, 1974

"Women beware. You are on the brink of destruction: You have hitherto been engaged in crushing your waists; now you are attempting to cultivate your mind. . . . Beware!! Science pronounces that the woman who studies is lost."
—DR. R. R. COLEMAN, late 1880s

"College does for girls what brandy does to hard sauce; it spoils the taste without adding a kick."
—NINA WILCOX PUTNAM, 1952

"When a woman inclines to learning, there is usually something wrong with her sex apparatus."
—FRIEDRICH NIETZSCHE

"The competitive woman destroys something in a man . . . a thing called self-respect."
—JUNE WILSON, syndicated columnist, 1960

"Men have more problems than women. In the first place, they have to put up with women."
—FRANÇOISE SAGAN

"I love men, not because they are men, but because they are not women."
—QUEEN CHRISTINA of Sweden

"I prefer a dumb man to an intelligent woman."
—BARBARA CARTLAND, 1977

"I don't think there's anything wrong about hitting a woman—although I don't recommend doing it in the same way you'd hit a man. An openhanded slap is justified—if all other alternatives fail and there has been plenty of warning."
—SEAN CONNERY, 1965

"A woman, a dog, and a walnut-tree,
The more you beat 'em the better they be."
—THOMAS FULLER (1608–1661)

"I had stepped outside of the white man's law, which I repudiated with scorn and self-satisfaction. I became a law unto myself—my own legislature, my own Supreme Court, my own executive. . . . Rape was an insurrectionary act."
—ELDRIDGE CLEAVER, *Soul on Ice* (1957)

"Any good whore knows more about sex than Betty Friedan."

—SAM PECKINPAH, 1972

"There is nothing enduring in life for a woman except what she builds in a man's heart."

—JUDITH ANDERSON, 1958

"The woman is expressly formed to please the man."

—JEAN JACQUES ROUSSEAU

"No man worth having is true to his wife, or can be true to his wife, or ever was or ever will be."

—SIR JOHN VANBRUGH

"Few women would want to thumb their noses at husbands, children, and community and go off on their own. Those who do may be talented individuals, but they rarely are successful women."

—*Redbook* magazine, 1960

"A woman is nobody. A wife is everything."

—*Philadelphia Public Ledger and Daily Transcript,* 1848

"The paramount mission and destiny of women are to fulfill the noble and benign offices of wife and mother. This is the law of the Creator."

—Supreme Court justice JOSEPH BRADLEY, 1873

"When we eliminated women from public life, it is because we want to give them back their essential honour. . . . The outstanding and highest calling of woman is always that of wife and mother and it would be an unthinkable misfortune if we allowed ourselves to be turned from this point of view."

—JOSEPH GOEBBELS, upholding the Nazi policy toward women

"The only good thing Mussolini did was to take away the right of women to vote."
     —TAYLOR CALDWELL, 1976

"Woman's creativeness has a direct soul-satisfying outlet in the bearing and rearing of children."
     —DR. BENJAMIN SPOCK, on why fewer women than men
     succeed in the arts, 1956

"If day care became widely available, it will be possible for a matriarchal social pattern to emerge. Under such conditions, however, the men will inevitably bolt. And this development . . . would probably require the simultaneous emergence of a police state to supervise the undisciplined men and a child care state to manage the children."
     —GEORGE GILDER, *Sexual Suicide* (1973)

"Approximately half the people in this world spend much of their lives under the raging hormonal imbalance of the periodic lunar cycle. In middle age, they escape this monthly madness at last, only to enter a different but equally unreliable state, characterized by curious mental aberrations. In this demented condition they continue to plague the planet for another twenty-five or thirty years. . . . Their physical and psychological disabilities render them unfit to make important decisions or hold positions of power. The only job for which they are truly qualified is bearing of young."
     —DR. EDGAR BERMAN, a member of the Democratic
     party's committee on national priorities, on why hor-
     mones should bar women from politics, 1972

"Athletic competition builds character in our boys. We do not need that kind of character in our girls."
     —A judge excluding a girl athlete from a school team on
     the basis of her sex, 1973

"We must not impute to a woman feelings in regard to the loss of her organs which are derived from what we, as men, would think of a similar operation on a man. A woman does not feel she is unsexed, and she is not unsexed."

—DR. E. W. CUSHING of Boston, of the popular "oophorectomies" (removal of ovaries) and "clitoridectomies" (removal of the clitoris) he performed on women to induce "normal" behavior, 1897

"We have to cultivate women's chastity as the highest national possession, for it is the only guarantee that we really are going to be the father of our children. . . . This, and not masculine selfishness, is the reason why the law and morals make stricter demands on the woman than on the man with regard to premarital chastity and to marital fidelity."

—MAX GRUBER, German sex hygienist, 1920s

"I'm all for women having equal rights. But I repeat, women shouldn't fight bulls because a bullfighter is and should be a man."

—PACO CAMINO, president of Spain's Bullfight Association

"Why don't you women stay home and be lovers and leave TV and football to the men?"

—Head coach JOHN MADDEN of the Oakland Raiders, denying CBS sportscaster Lee Arthur access to the practice field, 1972

"I'll agree that women are the equals of men when I see pregnant women in the paratroop corps."

—COLONEL MUAMMAR QADDAFI of Libya, quoted by Susan Sontag, 1976

"A man would be thought a coward who had no more courage than a courageous woman."

—ARISTOTLE

"What would they do with the chest protectors? Rebuild them all?"

> —EARLY WYNN, pitching coach for the Minnesota Twins, on the attempts of a New York woman to get a job as umpire in the major leagues, 1968

"While I am not saying that there is a necessary connection between baboon patterns and human patterns ... I am proposing that 'human nature' is such that it is 'unnatural' for females to engage in defense, police, and, by implication, high politics."

> —LIONEL TIGER, *Men in Groups* (1969)

"A woman is only a woman, but a good cigar is a Smoke."

> —RUDYARD KIPLING

"There is no equality except in a cemetery. There are differences in physical structure and biological function. . . . There is more difference between male and female than between a horse chestnut and a chestnut horse."
　　—EMANUEL CELLER, congressman, discussing the ERA, 1923

"It would be difficult for me to say I'm against working women when I've had a Champagne Lady on my show for nineteen years. . . . I like clean ladies and nice ladies."
　　—LAWRENCE WELK

CRITICS

"Shakespeare's words are too indecent to be translated."
—SAMUEL TAYLOR COLERIDGE, 1815

"I think Shakespeare is shit. Absolute shit! He may have been a genius for his time, but I just can't relate to that stuff. 'Thee' and 'thou'—the guy sounds like a faggot."
—GENE SIMMONS of the rock group Kiss

"If Beethoven's Seventh Symphony is not by some means abridged, it will soon fall into disuse."
—PHILIP HALE, Boston music critic, 1837

"These books are either in accordance with the teachings of the Koran or they are opposed to it. If in accord, then they are useless, since the Koran itself is sufficient, and if in opposition, they are pernicious and must be destroyed."
—OMAR, Arab leader and conqueror of Alexandria, on why he used the books from the famous Alexandrian library to heat the baths, 642 A.D.

"My whole point was to prove gossip can be literature."
> —TRUMAN CAPOTE, of a controversial *Esquire* article in which he blew the whistle on his society friends

"This will make Tolstoy's *War and Peace* look like a minor work."
> —JAMES DICKEY, novelist, of the two books he was writing simultaneously, 1977

"This film is apparently meaningless, but if it has any meaning it is doubtless objectionable."
> —British Board of Film Censors, on their decision to ban Jean Cocteau's *The Seashell and the Clergyman*, 1956

"I am not sure that if I understood the picture completely I would agree with what it is saying."
> —ARCHER WINSTON, film critic, at a New York film festival, 1966

"Profoundly unfair ... historically prejudiced ... profoundly anti-democratic and alien to any concept of the interests of the people. ..."
> —Soviet censors on Boris Pasternak's novel *Dr. Zhivago*

"Wagner's music is better than it sounds."
> —Humorist BILL NYE

"Modern music is as dangerous as cocaine."
> —PIETRO MASCAGNI (1863–1945)

"Rembrandt is not to be compared in the painting of character with our extraordinarily gifted English artist, Mr. Rippingille."
> —JOHN HUNT, nineteenth-century English critic

"Norman Lear is just like Thomas Hardy."
        —GAIL PARENT, 1978

"[*Roots* is] obviously great, ranking with the Bible and Homer's *Iliad* and *Odyssey.*"
        —ALEX HALEY, 1977

"Although written many years ago, *Lady Chatterley's Lover* has just been reissued . . . and this pictorial account of the day-by-day life of an English gamekeeper is full of considerable interest to outdoor minded readers, as it contains many passages on pheasant-raising, the apprehending of poachers, ways to control vermin, and other chores and duties of the professional gamekeeper. Unfortunately, one is obliged to wade through many pages of extraneous material in order to discover and savour these sidelights on the management of a midland shooting estate, and in this reviewer's opinion the book cannot take the place of J. R. Miller's *Practical Gamekeeping.*"
        —Review of *Lady Chatterley's Lover* in *Field and Stream*, c. 1959

"We are simply and solely gladdened by the spectacle of efflux which emanates from the perfect relation of parts to a whole within a given actual object."
        —JAMES K. FEIBLEMAN, critic

"We don't want to censor your songs. What we want to do is change your song. You're the younger generation; you believe in change."
        —ROCCO LAGINESTRA, president of RCA Records, quoted
        by Paul Kantner

LAW AND ORDER

"I was so busy with my work in court that I forgot to file my returns."
> —Judge NEVILLE TUCKER of Kentucky, on being arrested for failing to pay income taxes, c. 1975

"I will always feel terrible that our beautiful relationship had to end up in the courts."
> —MICHELLE TRIOLA MARVIN, of her palimony suit against actor Lee Marvin, 1977

"It shall be unlawful for any suspicious person to be within the municipality."
> —Local ordinance, Euclid, Ohio

"It is me, but I don't remember doing it."
> —Ku Klux Klansman JERRY PAUL SMITH at his trial for murder, watching a film that showed him firing into a crowd of Communist party members, 1980

"I'm convinced that every boy, in his heart, would rather steal second base than an automobile."
> —Supreme Court Justice TOM CLARK

"I'm gonna be tough as mayor. I'm gonna make Attila the Hun look like a faggot."
> —FRANK RIZZO of Philadelphia, elected mayor in 1971 on a strong anticrime platform

"I have no doubt that this man deliberately took poison and he appears to have done so in a most cold-blooded and heartless way."
> —A British coroner, summing up his testimony, 1937

"Where would Christianity be if Jesus got eight to fifteen years with time off for good behavior?"
> —New York State Senator JAMES H. DONOVAN, arguing in support of capital punishment

"We have seen more than once that the public welfare may call upon the best citizens for their lives. It would be strange if it could not call upon those who already sap the strength of the state for these lesser sacrifices. . . . Three generations of imbeciles are enough."
> —Supreme Court Justice OLIVER WENDELL HOLMES, JR., delivering the Court's decision upholding Virginia's sterilization law, 1928. The case involved the sterilization of a "feeble-minded" woman—whose mother had also been "feeble-minded"—and her two daughters. Neither of the two daughters, both alive in 1983, were really mentally deficient, but both are, of course, childless.

"If my name didn't end with a vowel, I wouldn't have had all this trouble."
> —FRANK SINATRA, complaining of his legal difficulties. A 1962 Justice Department memorandum reported its surveillance placed the singer in contact with ten of the country's top gangsters.

"There is no such thing as organized crime."
— MEYER LANSKY, 1978

"I never said I was tough on crime."
— EVELLE YOUNGER, California attorney general, discussing well-documented allegations that he was close to mob interests, 1978

"You can't blame a man for trying."
— Connecticut Judge WALTER PICKET, after dismissing a charge of conspiracy to rape

"Lay back and enjoy it."
— Police Captain RICHARD OLBERDING of Spokane, Washington, advising women on what to do if confronted by the rapist who was terrorizing the city, 1981

"I've struck a raw nerve but women *are* sex objects. God did that; I didn't."

> —County Judge ARCHIE SIMONSON of Madison, Wisconsin, who declared that a fifteen-year-old boy was reacting "morally" to community standards when he joined in an attack on a sixteen-year-old girl. Simonson was finally turned out of office by a campaign led by women, 1977.

"The policeman isn't there to create disorder. The policeman is there to *preserve* disorder."

> —Mayor RICHARD DALEY of Chicago, 1968

"Crack down on hoodlums; shoot their asses off."

> —JIMMY HOFFA

"Resist lovingly. . . . Resist spiritually, stay high . . . praise God . . . love life . . . blow the mechanical mind with Holy Acid. . . . Arm yourselves and shoot to live. . . . Life is never violent. To shoot a genocidal robot policeman in defense of life is a sacred act."

> —TIMOTHY LEARY

"The place is too corrupt for me."

> —FRANK COSTELLO, "prime minister of the underworld," explaining to Albert Anastasia why he wouldn't consider moving to New Jersey

"There are times when the President . . . would be right to disobey an order of the Supreme Court."

> —Texas Governor JOHN CONNALLY; he later qualified this statement by saying that, as President, the only Court decision he would disobey personally would be "an order to invade Latin America, or something like that."

"I can't seem to adjust to your society, because no matter what I do is wrong."

> —CHARLES MANSON, 1976

"If Robert Kennedy were alive today, he would not countenance singling me out for this kind of treatment."

> —SIRHAN SIRHAN, Kennedy's assassin, arguing for parole in 1984 from California's Soledad prison, 1983

"I snapped or something."

> —ORVALL WYATT LOYD of Dallas, explaining why he had hacked his mother-in-law to death after mistaking her for a large raccoon, 1981

"I don't approve of all this sleeping around. I don't understand it."

> —Attributed to JEAN HARRIS, commenting on the activities of her students

"Fishing [and] gardening."

> —Mafia "Boss of Bosses" CARMINE GALANTE, on his chief interests in life

"Those boys wouldn't know a good lawyer from a good watermelon."

> —Judge GERALD CULKIN, of the Manhattan-Bronx Supreme Court, on four black defendants, "the Harlem Four." Attorney William Kunstler was seeking permission for himself and another attorney to defend two of them. The remark earned Culkin a listing in a *New York* magazine article on "The Ten Worst Judges in New York" (1972).

"There seems to be no hope for rehabilitating you."

> —A Vancouver magistrate, deciding on a six-month jail term for a seventy-three-year-old prostitute

"[A black person] has no rights which a white man need respect."

> —Chief Justice ROGER TANEY, handing down the Supreme Court's decision in the Dred Scott case, 1857

"Good people, fine people from fine backgrounds, just don't kill people in cold blood."

>—DOUG SCHMIDT, defending his client, ex-city official Dan White, who killed San Francisco mayor George Moscone and city supervisor Harvey Milk

"The knife in my wife's belly was a crime. It was a grave crime, but it had nothing to do with violence."

>—NORMAN MAILER, discussing his attack on his second wife, Peruvian painter Adele Morales

"Is that criminal or illegal or un-American to try to help two young ladies build up equity?"

>—BOBBY BAKER, defending his purchase of a co-op apartment for his secretary/mistress Carole Tyler

"Brooms, etc. . . . . $41,190.95."

>—A bookkeeping entry in the account books of the corrupt Tweed Ring, which ran New York City, 1869

"Do not rely on your ability to speak 'off the cuff.' This is a foolhardy stunt that could prove disastrous to your client."

>—F. LEE BAILEY and HENRY B. ROTHBLATT, *Successful Techniques for Criminal Trials* (1971), p. 235

"[The final argument] that's where you win or lose. And I won't know what I'm going to say until I get to my feet. I never use notes. That is a terrible crutch."

>—F. LEE BAILEY, quoted in the *Los Angeles Times*, February 20, 1976

"When people around you treat you like a child and pay no attention to the things you say, you have to do *something*!"

>—LYNETTE "SQUEAKY" FROMME, explaining why she tried to gun down President Gerald Ford

"When one is a painter, but all one's ideas are already in the heads of others, what can one do?"

> —JEAN-JACQUES MONTFORT, Europe's greatest living art forger, who has spent four years in prison, 1978

"At the time, it did not seem important enough."

> —GENERAL AUGUSTE MERCIER, French minister of war, on why he assured the conviction of Alfred Dreyfus (1894) by not showing him the phony "secret" evidence against him

"I hated to do it."

> —FATHER DIVINE (George Baker), commenting on the heart attack death of Judge Lewis J. Smith who, four days previously, had sentenced the religious cult leader to prison, 1932. Divine claimed to be God incarnate; Smith had previously been in good health.

BEAUTY
AND FASHION

"Vanity is healthy."
　　　—Ivo Pintangui, one of the world's most popular plastic
　　　surgeons

"I've always, all my life, pitied those poor people who
have to buy the Thom McAn kind of shoes. Because after
they have bought six pairs of shoes, they would have been
better off to buy just one really good pair."
　　　—Pauline Trigère

"If you adore her, you must adorn her. There lies the essence of a happy marriage."
　　　—Anne Fogarty, *Wife Dressing* (1959)

"Elegance is clean nails and clean hair, the way you talk
and the way you move. Elegance is also your shoes, beautiful underwear, the sheets you sleep in, the way you keep

your handbag. It's a sense of quality. It's being consistent, and it's even the kind of watch you keep next to your bed."
—GLORIA GUINNESS, *Harper's Bazaar,* March 1973

"This part is never to be seen. It is bone and I do not find bone attractive."
—CHRISTIAN DIOR, on why he banished knees, 1957

"He created nudity."
—DIANA VREELAND, of Halston

"If you practice discipline, the tummy gets the message and shrinks. . . ."
—LUCIANA AVEDON, *The Beauty Book* (1971)

"Women are emotionally hungry for the experience of wearing a short skirt."
—BETSEY JOHNSON, designer, 1981

"We've seen the heyday of hair. Now we're in ramu with the shape of the head."
—KENNETH, 1968 (Ramu, Sumerian for *love,* was the name of the hairdresser's new fragrance.)

"Of typical good family, a little hollow-chested. She can wear a slightly vulgar dress since she exhales good family through every pore of her body."
—GUY PAULIN, owner/designer of Paraphernalia boutique, on the ideal customer for his see-through clothes, 1969

"Choosing perfume is one of a woman's most personal forms of expression because it reflects who you are."
—BIANCA JAGGER, 1977

"The fact is you can get away with anything—even creamed tuna à la king—if you do it with panache. Serve the tuna accompanied by *Symphonies and Fanfares for a King's Supper.* . . . It is a perfect feast of Couperin and Lully—and the music is played with all the splendor it had when Louis XIV's court musicians performed it at his 100-course repasts."

> —*Harper's Bazaar*, "How to Stretch Your Dollars and Have Lots of Good Health, Good Looks, Good Fun," February 1975

"The Independent Woman is past carrying placards and yelling for her rights. Now she can be comfortable and confident about her femininity. She has a new image of herself—and it takes a variety of fragrances to keep up with her. She'll wear Charlie to quicken her pace and Jontue to quicken her pulse, Norell when she wants to feel particularly elegant."

> —PAUL WOOLARD, president of Cosmetics and Fragrances, Revlon, U.S.A., 1976

"There are some people who have the disjointed notion of believing a hairdresser is a person of service."

> —JON PETERS, companion of Barbra Streisand, 1974

"From Russia, our Paragon Traveller . . . reported that during her investigation of Moscow and Leningrad, she lunched and dined and thrived every day on *caviar, orange juice, and ice cream.* 'Purely from passion,' she admitted. 'These three items just happen to be the most delicious things to eat there. . . . Frankly, I never felt better. And my nails and hair grew with enormous speed.'"

> —*Vogue* Beauty Bulletin, September 15, 1968

"If I really want to be fantastically beautiful, I lie down for half of an hour and I concentrate to be beautiful."

> —VERUSCHKA, top model of the sixties, 1968

"With my new dress form I have discarded, among other things, the limitations set by the shape of the female figure itself."

> —HUBERT DE GIVENCHY, describing the "sack" dress, a baglike shape he created and ballyhooed, 1957. But by 1958 the never-popular "sack" was passé.

"Rips and tears are as valid ways to handle fabric as pleating is. And chains and safety pins are simply alternative, nontraditional decoration for the seventies."

> —ZANDRA RHODES, designer, on her ripped and pinned clothes, 1977

"I love the sexy gleam of softly frosted shadow, especially offbeat colors like prune or yellow. Yellow is fabulous."

> —PABLO, makeup artist at Elizabeth Arden, on the best colors for "evening eyes," 1971

"It's a bad joke that won't last. Not with winter coming."

> —COCO CHANEL, on the miniskirt, 1966

"In 1970, in addition to the illnesses, the poverty and the dead, just to have something new to worry about we had pollution, and the fear of another war. But in spite of it all, and God alone knows how, we kept our cool, and somehow or other got rid of the miniskirt."

> —GLORIA GUINNESS, 1970

"Stop blaming me! Paris created the midi. We just reported on it. That's all we did. And if we happened to influence manufacturers and store owners, it wasn't the newspaper's fault."

> —JOHN FAIRCHILD, publisher of *Women's Wear Daily*, on the failure of the midi which he had "decreed" as the hit of 1970 and promoted in his paper. The longer length failed to catch on and many retailers suffered from having followed his advice.

"Why don't you . . .
Sweep into the drawing room on your first big night with an enormous red fox muff of many skins?

Remember how delicious champagne cocktails are after tennis or golf? Indifferent champagne can be used for these.

Wear bare knees and long white knitted socks, as Unity Mitford does when she takes tea with Hitler at the Carlton in Munich?

Rinse your blond child's hair in dead champagne to keep its gold, as they do in France?"

> —DIANA VREELAND, some helpful suggestions in one of her "Why Don't You" columns which, beginning in 1936, ran for decades in *Harper's Bazaar*

"To illustrate that anything goes these days as long as you're discreet."

> —JAMES BRADY, editor of *Harper's Bazaar,* on the close-up photo he had planned to use of two women kissing on the mouth, 1971. Hearst management insisted that the picture be pulled shortly before the magazine went to press, at a cost of thousands of dollars.

"Of course, if you're really into fashion you'll want our Chinese-worker jacket in denim, there's even a matching collar and lead, and for your more formal occasions we suggest a red or grey Chesterfield with black velvet collar. A navy blazer is nice for milder days and on rainy ones you might fancy yourself in our private-eye trench coat. Needless to say, we have collars and leads to complement each of your outfits, including our warmest winter storm coats."

> —Letter from Saks Fifth Avenue's Dog Toggery to dogs on its mailing list, 1976

SEX

"There's two ways to release tension. Either through violence or sex. It saddens me that we've decided to take the violence route."

> —LARRY FLYNT, publisher of *Hustler,* on the moral superiority of pornography, 1977

"No worthwhile interest for soldiers."

> —U.S. Army, banning the Kinsey report from army post exchanges in West Germany, 1953

"It is wrong to suggest that we favor depersonalized sex—unless, by depersonalized sex we are referring to any and all sexual activity that does not include extensive involvement, commitment and obligations. . . ."

> —HUGH HEFNER

"[As] American as cherry pie."

> —EDWARD M. BRECHER, of group sex, in his book *The Sex Researchers* (1969)

"Love between man and woman is a psychosomatic activity which consumes energy and wastes time. On the other hand, love of the Chairman takes no time at all, and is in itself a powerful tonic."

—*The Peking Workers' Daily*

"The kind of knowledge that is picked up through illicit relations is likely to have to be unlearned."

—LOUISE FOX CONNELL, "A Woman's Responsibility in Sex Relations," *Reader's Digest,* July 1942

"A boy must not indulge himself in his youth if he wants to become a coherent, secure adult. He might keep in mind that gluttons don't enjoy the taste of food."

—MARION HILLIARD, *A Woman Doctor Looks at Life and Love*

"What I like about swinging is that no thought processes are going on."

—"A swinger," lauding orgies in an article by Richard Warren

"Group sex could jeopardize a relationship and it could enhance it— Again, it all depends on your attitude. If a woman is very jealous, then she'd better not engage in group sex. Or perhaps she'd better, in order to work on her jealousy."

—DR. SHIRLEY ZUSSMAN

"Preferably I would not want my daughters in there, but not because I think it's wrong."

—JOE CONFORTE, brothel owner, when asked whether he would encourage his daughters to go into that line of work

"Cats know that sort of thing without having to be toilet trained."

—DR. GORDON V. DRAKE, opponent of sex education, indicating that toilet training is one of its sins, 1968

"It is nothing more than sex education, essential and necessary in his growth toward maturity and subsequent domestic family life."
—Ruling of a Santa Fe judge in an incest case

"[The] victim of masturbation passes from one degree of imbecility to another, till all of the powers of the system, mental, physical and moral, are blotted out forever."
—THE REVEREND JOHN TODD, 1870s

"I do not think that masturbation is a bad thing; for the first time women are shown involved with their bodies, which is what the women's movement is all about."
—CHRISTIE HEFNER, *Playboy* executive, responding to criticism that the magazine was demeaning women by showing a nude woman with a finger on her clitoris

"I see myself as a humanitarian, whatever that means."
—CAROL DODA, who became the first topless dancer in 1964

"I'm very educational. Earl Wilson said I'm the most educational woman he's ever talked to."
—MONICA KENNEDY, one of America's foremost stripteasers

"In the U.S.S.R. . . . since private property and capital have been abolished, love is free of all . . . material considerations, and adultery no longer exists."
—A Soviet sociologist

"If paternity leave were granted it would result in a direct incitement to a population explosion."
—IAN GOW, British member of Parliament, 1979

"You taught us not to hide our feelings."
—LARRY FLYNT, in a full page ad in *The New York Times* announcing his prayer vigil for Senator Hubert Humphrey, December 18, 1977

"The woman has even more to lose when she sees sex as natural for herself as a female animal. She loses the possibility of the devotion and care of a good man throughout her life. She loses the likelihood of a home of her own. She loses her reputation, her standing, her status among respectable people everywhere. She loses the feeling of being personally worthy. In time, as she ages, she loses even her temporary male companions, as they turn to younger sex partners."
> —EVELYN MILLIS DUVALL, *Why Wait Till Marriage?* (1965)

"The normal woman derives her keenest pleasure from surrender, while the healthy male gets his from dominance."
> —THE REVEREND MARGARET BLAIR JOHNSTONE, "What Those I Counsel Don't Know About Sex," *Reader's Digest,* January 1953

"We want to take the erotic film out of the hands of the smut peddlers and give it some class."
> —KEN GAUL, co-director of the First Annual New York Erotic Film Festival, 1972

"In males, one of the most general physical causes of sexual excitement is constipation. . . . When this condition is chronic, as in habitual constipation, the unnatural excitement often leads to serious results."
> —DR. J. H. KELLOGG, 1879

"I don't hate homosexuals. I love homosexuals. It's the sin of homosexuality I hate."
> —ANITA BRYANT, 1977. Following her divorce, which destroyed her image as the perfect family woman, Bryant commented, "The answers don't seem quite so simple now. . . ."

"I don't know. I never met one."
> —BILLY GRAHAM, when asked whether he thought a homosexual would make a good minister, 1975

"I know of no homosexuals in the NHL. We are remarkably free of that stuff, thank God."

> —FRANK TORPEY, National Hockey League security director, after a player's revelations, 1976

"They are trying to achieve a feeling of unity."

> —Minister at a Jones Beach sunrise wedding ceremony at which the bride and groom made love in front of the startled guests, 1970

"I should say that the majority of women (happily for society) are not much troubled with sexual feeling of any kind."

> —DR. WILLIAM ACTON, 1857

"[Women embrace their husbands] without a particle of sex desire."

> —DR. MARY WOOD-ALLEN, nineteenth-century physician

"A man can feel kinship with the gods if his wife can make him believe he can cause a flowering within her. If she doesn't feel it she must bend every effort to pretend. This is the worthiest duplicity on earth; I heartily recommend it to discontented wives."

> —MARION HILLIARD, *A Woman Doctor Looks at Love and Life*

Playboy interviewer: "We've heard that some women who ordinarily have difficulty achieving orgasm find themselves capable of multiple orgasms under LSD. Is that true?"

Dr. Timothy Leary: "In a carefully prepared, loving LSD session a woman will inevitably have several hundred orgasms."

Playboy: "Several *hundred?*"

Leary: "Yes. Several hundred."

> —*Playboy* interview, September 1962. This claim proved to be pure baloney; like most drugs, LSD is an anaphrodisiac.

"To be sexually attracted to a being who belongs to a different class which is hostile and morally alien to one's own is just as much a *perversion* as it would be to feel sexual attraction for a crocodile or an orangutang."

>—ZALKIND, a Soviet psychologist, *Youth and Revolution* (1925)

"Sex without class consciousness cannot give satisfaction, even if it is repeated until infinity."

>—ALDO BRANDIRALI, secretary-general of the Italian Marxist-Leninist party, stating the party's official guidelines for sex in a manual, 1973

"No woman should be kept on the Pill for twenty years until, in fact, a sufficient number have been kept on the Pill for twenty years."

>—SIR ALAN STERLING PARKS, 1970

"The publication of *Eros* [magazine] represents a major breakthrough in the battle for the liberation of the human spirit."

>—RALPH GINZBURG, in promotional material for his erotic magazine *Eros,* 1965

"[The Cardinal's aid] extended often to the most disreputable and downtrodden persons."

>—The Episcopal Council of the French Catholic Church, after the death of Jean Cardinal Daniélou in the Paris apartment of a blond stripper whose husband was in jail for pimping, 1974

"After being alive, the next hardest work is sex. . . . Some people *get* energy from sex and some people *lose* energy from sex. I have found that it's too much work. But if you have the time for it, and if you need the exercise—then you should do it."

>—ANDY WARHOL

SCIENCE

"I have not held and do not hold as true the opinion which has been condemned, of the motion of the Earth, and the stability of the Sun. . . ."

> —GALILEO, disavowing his theory, at his trial before the Inquisition, 1633

"There is no likelihood man can ever tap the power of the atom. The glib supposition of utilizing atomic energy when our coal has run out is a completely unscientific Utopian dream, a childish bug-a-boo. Nature has introduced a few foolproof devices into the great majority of elements that constitute the bulk of the world, and they have no energy to give up in the process of disintegration."

> —DR. ROBERT MILLIKAN, Nobel Prize winner, 1923

"Why the greatest invention in history is the safety pin. The second greatest is perforated toilet paper."

> —TINY TIM, 1970

"The energy produced by the breaking down of the atom is a very poor kind of thing. Anyone who looks for a source of power in the transformation of the atom is talking moonshine."
—SIR ERNEST RUTHERFORD, 1933

"A very few individuals working a few hours a day at very easy tasks in the central atomic power plant will provide all the heat, light, and power required by the community, and these utilities will be so cheap that their cost can hardly be reckoned."
—ROBERT M. HUTCHINS, chancellor of the University of Chicago, predicting the near future of atomic energy, 1945

"Other difficulties I do not foresee that could prevail against this invention, save one only, which to me seems the greatest of them all, and that is that God would never surely allow such a machine to be successful."
—FRANCESCO LANA, proposing the construction of a "flying canoe," 1670

"Heavier-than-air flying machines are impossible."
—WILLIAM THOMSON, Lord Kelvin, president of the Royal Society (1890–95)

"Rail travel at high speed is not possible, because passengers, unable to breathe, would die of asphyxia."
—DR. DIONYSUS LARDNER (1793–1859), professor of natural philosophy and astronomy at University College, London. Lardner also predicted that no large steamship would be able to cross the Atlantic—two years before the feat was performed.

"Aside from being tremendous it was one of the most aesthetically beautiful things I have ever seen."
—DONALD HORNIG, on the first atomic test

"We stand ready to furnish a practical machine for use in war at once. . . . We are only waiting to complete arrangements with some government. The American government has apparently decided to permit foreign governments to take the lead in utilizing our invention for war purposes. We greatly regret this attitude of our own country, but see no way to remedy it; we have made a formal proposition to the British government and expect to have a conference with one of its representatives, at Dayton, very soon."
—WILBUR WRIGHT, 1905

"When my brother and I built and flew the first man-carrying flying machine, we thought that we were introducing into the world an invention which would make further wars practically impossible."
—ORVILLE WRIGHT, 1917

"In about three years commercial planes will fly from New York to California in one hour."
—DR. ALEXANDER W. LIPPISCH, U.S. Air Force researcher, 1948

"It's very simple. Any undergraduate physics major could have done what I did."
—JOHN ARISTOTLE PHILLIPS, Princeton student who designed an atomic bomb in a physics class, 1976

"To place a man in a multi-stage rocket and project him into the controlling gravitational field of the moon, where the passenger can make scientific observations, perhaps land alive, and then return to earth—all that constitutes a wild dream worthy of Jules Verne."
—LEE DE FOREST, electronics pioneer, 1957

"I find it difficult to believe that the seat belt can afford the driver any great amount of protection over and above that which is available to him through the medium of the safety-type steering wheel if he has his hands on the wheel and grips the rim sufficiently tight to take advantage of its energy absorption properties and also takes advantage of the shock-absorbing action which can be achieved by correct positioning of the feet and legs."

> —HOWARD GANDELOT, vehicle safety engineer for General Motors, 1954

"I feel absolutely certain that the United States won't put a man on the moon. The moon won't hold up a man. It's a soggy mass. They'll get in close proximity, but they'll never boil a cup of tea on it."

> —"HARRIET," a psychic, prediction in the *Chicago Sun-Times,* December 1968

"Hang up! Look what happened to the Indians."

> —DR. ALBERT HIBBS of Caltech's Jet Propulsion Laboratory, when asked how we should reply to the first message from another world via UFOs

"The Air Force is *not* hiding any UFO information. And I do not qualify this in any way."

> —Assistant Secretary of the Air Force RICHARD E. HORNER, 1958. Actually, in 1947 the Air Force had created UFO Project Sign, a directive for secrecy on the subject.

"I expect him to do extremely well and to live a long time."

> —DR. MICHAEL DEBAKEY, after removing the cancerous spleen of the shah of Iran in Cairo, Egypt, April 1980

"Those still alive at the age of eighty are more intelligent than those who died."

> —*American Medical News* report of an IQ longevity study made by a Philadelphia Geriatric Center, 1970

"Most Medicaid bookkeeping is a fallacy."

> —DR. WILLIAM TRIEBEL, on the U.S. Senate report that described him as the "highest-billing Medicaid physician in the nation." Triebel ran three methadone clinics which took in $785,114 in 1975 from the New York State Medicaid program, but the doctor claimed that he and his wife had netted only $30,000.

"[Elvis] was not abusing drugs."

> —DR. GEORGE NICHOPOULOS of Memphis, physician to Presley, shortly after his death, 1977

"It was never really effective, but it helped psychologically because the people who used it didn't know it wasn't effective."

> —DR. C. SCOTT JOHNSON of the San Diego Naval Undersea Center, discussing a chemical shark repellant in use by the military since World War II

"Einstein's theory is unnecessary."

> —HAROLD ASPDEN, *Physics Without Einstein* (1969)

BUSINESS

"This company is not bust. We are merely in a cyclical decline."

—LORD STOKES, chairman of British Leyland, 1974

"We are in a period of negative economic growth."

—THOMAS MURPHY, president of General Motors, explaining the slump in auto sales, 1980

"It isn't that we build such bad cars; it's that they are such lousy customers."

—CHARLES F. KETTERING, president and chairman of the board of General Motors (1925–49)

"Problems are the price of progress. Don't bring me anything but trouble. Good news weakens me."

—CHARLES F. KETTERING

"God runs Tiffany's."

—WALTER HOVING, president of Tiffany's

"I'm not a hustler, I'm not an entrepreneur. I didn't get into the Gilmore thing to make money. It was very hard for me to watch the execution. Do you know I had to go to the bathroom thirteen times that morning?"

> —LARRY SCHILLER, agent of sensational events and peddler of the Gary Gilmore execution photos to *Playboy* magazine, 1977. His "packages" have included the deathbed confession of Jack Ruby (turned into an LP) and rights to the final nude photos of Marilyn Monroe.

"Banks are here to help the people who want to come up in the world."

> —DAVID ROCKEFELLER, 1976

"The rules of the United States are not necessarily the best rules to follow. What is wrong in one country, according to its traditions, evolution and morality, may be okay in another. In many countries it is the accepted policy to pay for expediting."

> —A. W. "TOM" CLAUSEN, president of Bank of America, world's largest bank, on the necessity for business payoffs abroad, 1977

"I would say anything done to get a favour is morally wrong."

> —ADNAN KHASHOGGI, in a TV interview, 1976. He is a Saudi Arabian middleman and billionaire—friend of Richard Nixon, Bebe Rebozo, and Robert Vesco—who received $106 million in fees and commissions from Lockheed Corporation. Questions about these transactions eventually led to trials in Japan and Italy.

"If you have to pay money to have the right thing done, it is only just and fair to do it."

> —COLLIS HUNTINGTON, promoter of the Central Pacific Railroad, on his obligation to pay off legislators. Between 1862 and 1873 Huntington's railroad spent some $1.9 million on "the right thing."

"Corporations are people too."

> —Secretary of the Treasury WILLIAM SIMON, advocating a tax break for big business

"What use would this company make of an electrical toy?"

> —Western Union president ORTON, to the infant Bell Telephone Company, which had offered all of its rights to Western Union for $100,000

"Nothing has come along that can beat the horse and buggy."

> —CHAUNCEY DEPEW, president of the New York Central Railroad, warning his nephew not to invest $5,000 in the new company started by Henry Ford

"Grow, industry, grow, grow, grow! Harmony and sincerity! Matsushita Electric!

> —Company song of Japan's Matsushita Electric Company

"Let the buyer beware; that covers the whole business. You cannot wet-nurse people from the time they are born until the time they die. They have got to wade in and get stuck, and that is the way men are educated and cultivated."

> —HENRY HAVEMEYER, of the American Sugar Refining Company, arguing early in the century that government should not protect the public against any corporation or product

"Women on certain jobs are every bit as good as men. We wouldn't think of having a man sell brassieres."

> —DRUMMOND BELL, vice-president of Montgomery Ward

"I think that if it were ever conclusively shown that there was some connection between smoking and, say, lung cancer, most agencies would not be advertising cigarettes. But it's easy to get stampeded, and the tobacco industry is being very much maligned. . . . The fact is that I have never met a finer group in my life than the people in the tobacco industry. . . . And tobacco has given pleasure to an awful lot of people. You should not act on hunches, suspicions, and stir-ups."

> —HENRY PATTISON, executive in charge of the Philip Morris account at the Benton and Bowles Advertising Agency, 1969

"Gosh, we're awed at how a story can be told and retold by the anti-cigarette people, and how little attention is given in the press to claims *for* cigarettes."

> —JAMES C. BOWLING, assistant to the president of Philip Morris

"Hell, there's more nitrates in a kiss than in a ton of bacon."

> —LARRY LEE, communications director of the National Pork Producers' Council

"Our food contains only the purest artificial preservatives."

> —Sign in a Manhattan restaurant, 1972

"I remember an American said there is more upset to the ozone layer by cows breaking wind than by a whole fleet of supersonic transports flying simultaneously."

> —ARCHIBALD RUSSELL, designer of the Concorde airplane, 1976

"I can assure you he was a normal man. Just like you and me."

> —CHUCK WALDRON, Howard Hughes's aide, scoffing at suggestions that Hughes may have been mentally ill

"I can afford $100,000 a year for twenty-five years, but no more than that. I don't want to get into a business that's going to lose money permanently."

> —SAM GORDON, Sacramento businessman, after stating
> that he'd be willing to lose money in order to get a Pacific
> Coast League baseball franchise for his city, 1968

"What is good for the country is good for General Motors, and what's good for General Motors is good for the country."

> —CHARLES E. WILSON, president of General Motors, to a
> congressional committee, 1952

"The average man won't really do a day's work unless he is caught and cannot get out of it. There is plenty of work to do, if people would do it."

> —HENRY FORD; five months after making this remark in
> the early 1930s he closed down his Detroit factories, thus
> almost completely relieving 75,000 more workers of their
> nagging obligation.

"The automobile business has lost its masculinity."

> —JOHN DELOREAN, upon leaving General Motors in 1972

"I really want to give the rest of my life to working in areas that are important to the country. . . . I must be working twice as hard as I did before. But no amount of money or success remotely approaches the feeling you get inside from doing a good thing for somebody."

> —JOHN DELOREAN, 1973

"You can always find something to change and tack the extra money onto. That's contract nourishment."

> —An air force plant representative at General Electric

"I think there is a world market for about five computers."

> —THOMAS J. WATSON, founder of IBM

"This is rat eat rat, dog eat dog. I'll kill 'em, and I'm going to kill 'em before they kill me. You're talking about the American way of survival of the fittest."

> —RAY KROC, founder of the McDonald's chain, explaining the code of the "self-made" man, 1972

"It requires a certain kind of mind to see beauty in a hamburger bun. Yet, is it any more unusual to find grace in the texture and softly curved silhouette of a bun than to reflect lovingly on . . . the arrangement of textures and colors in a butterfly's wing?"

> —RAY KROC

"The individual choice of garnishment of a burger can be an important point to the consumer in this day when individualism, in my mind, is an increasingly important thing to people."
>—DONALD N. SMITH, president of Burger King

"Maybe I'll become the Colonel Sanders of beer."
>—BILLY CARTER, on the launching of Billy Beer in 1977. It flopped.

"It wasn't a romantic relationship."
>—MARY ELIZABETH CUNNINGHAM, on her friendship with William Agee, chairman of Bendix Corporation, 1980. She was his executive assistant, quickly went to vice-president for strategic planning. When rumors about the pair broke, she resigned; they have since wed.

"When a record is recorded in front of three million people by anyone who has his kind of influence and prestige, it doesn't hurt to have that kind of representation in your company."
>—RON ALEXENBURG, president of Infinity Records, commenting on his release of a recording by Pope John Paul II

"How in the world can you expect a congressman or a senator to stay on Capitol Hill and do his job and still run out and make speeches and do his campaigning? There are times you can't depend on commercial airlines because of the time involved."
>—DITA BEARD, Washington lobbyist for ITT, on why she was always ready to provide congressmen with such harmless free services as trips on ITT planes—"I'm just an old mother." Beard was the focus of a 1972 controversy over the alleged settlement of an antitrust suit against ITT in return for a $400,000 donation to the Republican campaign.

"I don't put anything in writing. If it's important enough, you shouldn't, and if it is not important enough, why bother?"

> —DITA BEARD, explaining her lack of possibly incriminating records

"There's no way to sell a book about an unknown Dutch painter."

> —The sales department of Doubleday and Company, turning down Irving Stone's first book, *Lust for Life* (about Vincent van Gogh). The book was put out by another publisher in 1934 and became a best-seller.

"It's terrible the way those boys don't have a chance. It's different for the girls there—they can go right into the brothel system . . . but the boys don't have a chance. We have to do something for them."

> —BERNIE CORNFELD, "wonder" entrepreneur of the 1960s, on why his foundation would support a home for orphan boys on Taiwan

"We wanted something for working people who didn't have time to dress but wanted to show their condolences and sympathy. It's nice to have someone care."

> —ALVIN VERRETTE, president of the Point Coupee Funeral Home in New Roads, Louisiana, who introduced the world's first drive-in funeral, 1977. Motorists were able to look at the casket through a picture window and sign a guest registry, without leaving their cars.

"The Con Ed system is in the best shape in fifteen years, and there's no problem about the summer."

> —CHARLES FRANK LUCE, chairman of Consolidated Edison, a few hours before the blackout in New York City, July 1977

"Rising unemployment figures, it seems, were inevitably reducing our market, yet we refused to be intimidated by this. Consideration of the matter showed that even those who drew unemployment benefits represented a potential market and one likely to be productive enough if approached in the right way. So instead of neglecting the unemployed we visualised them as a prospective market of 2,500,000 people."

—Representative of a British tonic wine firm, 1931

"I see a lot of Ford products running around the streets, so you people must know what you're doing."

—Unidentified dealer, who signed up for an Edsel dealership in 1957 without seeing the car

"If no changes are made, either by Congress or EPA, we will not be able to build cars after late 1974 because we will not be able to meet the standards."

—HENRY FORD, II, on why pollution standards would finish the auto industry

"It's of the same order as the hula hoop—a fad. Six months from now, we'll probably be on another kick."

—W. B. MURPHY, president of the Campbell Soup Company, observing that public concern over auto safety would probably be short-lived, 1966

"In Brazil the present generation didn't receive any political or social education. So we provide them with a mechanism for protest; it is a protest through consumption."

—ROBERT ORSI, Pepsi-Cola Company, Brazil

"Although her father is president-director of the company, Nathalie enjoys no special privileges."

—*Harper's Bazaar* on Nathalie Hocq, manager of Cartier-Paris, in an article on working women who made it to the top, November 1975

"I consider it my patriotic duty to keep Elvis in the ninety percent tax bracket."

> —COLONEL TOM PARKER, upon the departure of his client, Elvis Presley, for the armed forces

"[Fishing] promotes a clean mind, healthy body and leaves no time for succumbing to Communistic or Socialistic propaganda."

> —IVAR HENNINGS, chairman, South Bend Bait Company, 1949

"Uninterrupted scenery, too, can get pretty monotonous. [McDonald's arches are] only a way of humanizing what is still an overwhelming landscape."

> —JUNE MARTINO, McDonald's executive, in a 1959 letter to *Fortune* magazine defending the chain against charges that it was defacing the highways

"We should not fall prey to the beautification extremists who have no sense of economic reality."

> —FRED L. HARTLEY, president of the Union Oil Company

"As long as humans know their signs and understand themselves better through astrology, I thought dogs should have their chance too."

> —GENEVIEVE CERF, who with her husband founded Caniscope, the first astrology service for dogs, 1975. Among the clients—canines belonging to Happy Rockefeller, Dustin Hoffman, and Gerald Ford.

"We are bringing the Bible to life. We are presenting Christ, presenting Jonah, presenting the characters of the Bible—bringing them to life, and letting them be as well-known as . . . Mickey Mouse or Donald Duck!"

> —BILL CAYWOOD of Holyland USA, a theme park in California modeled on Disneyland

"People have seen the light."

> —GEORGE MCLAIN, bishop of the Universal Life Church, on his scheme to sign people up with the church so that they could declare their property tax-exempt, 1976. He ordained 1,525 people in the Livingston, New York, area.

"Do not use the word 'contract.' Use the word 'agreement.' And don't ask the prospect if he wants the lot. Ask him a question and write the answer on your agreement. Ask, 'What is your correct name, sir? What is your correct mailing address?' And so on through the agreement. Remember, if he has let you fill out the agreement, *he has bought.* Okay, what do you do when you get to the bottom? Don't ask him to sign. You know what's wrong with the word 'sign?' You have been taught all your life to read every word, be careful, beware, don't sign anything. So you ask him to *okay* the agreement. He won't sign it but he will *okay* it."

> —A sales memo on selling land, quoted in *The Great Land Hustle* by James O. Foote (1972)

BUREAUCRACY

"Don't quote me as saying that we will or we should increase our external aid. That would be an opinion if I had an opinion, but as a member of my government I don't have an opinion."
> —PAUL MARTIN, Canadian external affairs minister, to the Toronto press on the question of foreign aid, 1965

"The President is aware of what is going on. That's not to say something is going on."
> —RON ZIEGLER, Nixon's press secretary, responding to a newsman's question

"This is an operative statement. The others are inoperative."
> —RON ZIEGLER, covering the inaccuracy of earlier Watergate statements, April 17, 1973

"There's a hope that some of the cross-roughing will be done earlier . . . that decisions will be broadly based . . . that we can increase inputs. . . . We need a process of involvement . . . a synthesization. . . . We've got to look at how problems interlink, the monitoring and the execution. . . . When there's an uncontrollable problem, that's the point in time when we must have analysis before we have ad hoc action."
>   —ALONZO MCDONALD, JR., leading management consultant and deputy to Carter aide Hamilton Jordan, 1979

"The College is committed to a consultative process of decision making in Academic affairs in an attempt to minimize the possibility of conflict inherent in a hierarchical structure and to maximize the opportunity for cooperative participation in constructive decision making. The Faculty has primary leadership in the formulation of all academic policies, which, through systematic procedures of consultation among all interested groups, are ultimately established by the Board of Trustees. The role of Dean of Faculty in this context is not to make the final decisions regarding policy determination but rather to strengthen the consultative process by coordinating the activities of Faculty and Administration, facilitating communication, and providing necessary information."
>   —Ad placed in *The New York Times* by the Search Committee for Dean of Faculty of St. Mary's College, Maryland

"Fifty million paper clips were issued [last year] and a large percentage of those probably were discarded too soon."
>   —Postmaster General LAWRENCE O'BRIEN in a bulletin to employees, 1966

"The appropriate concepts of cost and gain depend upon the level of optimization, and the alternative policies that are admissible. This appropriate level of optimization and the alternatives that should be compared depend in part on the search for a suitable criterion."

> —Department of the Interior, interoffice memo

"The one we had has only one table."

> —ARTHUR BRILL, Justice Department spokesman, explaining the installation of a second private dining room in the offices of the department, 1982

"Well, you know how it is, nobody's human."

> —ALBERT HALL, assistant secretary of defense for intelligence, commenting on why so many intelligence agencies gather the same information

"The character of the discussions inevitably is entirely different when the President of the United States talks than when an assistant talks who cannot make any definite statement. The basic objective of this trip was to set in motion a train of events and an evolution in the policy of our two countries which both sides recognized would be slow at first and present many difficulties in which a great deal depended on the assessment by each side of the understanding by the other of what was involved in this process and of the assessment by each side of the reliability of the other in being able to pursue this for the amount of time necessary to see it prevail. In this sense it almost had to be conducted by the heads of the two Governments and in this sense I would say that in the depth and seriousness of the discussions it went obviously beyond what had been discussed in my visits and beyond our expectations."

> —HENRY KISSINGER, asked for a report on President Nixon's trip to Peking, 1972

"Federal Highway Administrator F. C. Turner ... testified that the environmental impact statements required by the National Environmental Policy Act will add approximately eighteen million pages of paperwork annually to the burden of his department. But is this so bad? Do we count the flakes of snow that give beauty and a sense of serenity to the countryside in winter? Do we count the drops of rain and shovel-loads of fertilizer that nurture the flowers that brighten our lives and the crops that provide us with food? To move into the numbers game is to establish an impersonal body count in a needless war against bureaucracy."

> —Bureaucrat JAMES BOREN, in a tongue-in-cheek statement before a congressional committee looking into red tape. Boren is president of the National Association of Professional Bureaucrats, an organization that promotes the development of ever-greater bureaucracy.

LOVE THY NEIGHBOR

"We [the Caucasians] are the first race in the world, and the more of the world we inherit the better it is for the human race."
—CECIL RHODES

"Race is everything. . . . Literature, science, art, in a word, civilization, depend on it. . . . The Saxons . . . are the only race which truly comprehends the meaning of the word liberty. . . . The source of all evil lies in the race, the Celtic race of Ireland."
—JOHN M. KEMBLE, English historian, 1849

"[Only the] Nordics propagate themselves successfully."
—CALVIN COOLIDGE

"God has not been preparing the English-speaking and Teutonic peoples for a thousand years for nothing but vain and idle self-contemplation and self-admiration. No!

He has made us the master organizers of the world to establish system where chaos reigns. . . . He has made us
adept in government that we may administer government
among savage and senile people. . . . He has marked the
American people as His chosen nation to finally lead in
the regeneration of the world. . . ."
> —Senator ALBERT J. BEVERIDGE, statement on the princi-
> ple of Manifest Destiny, 1900

"I don't see much future for the Americans. Everything
about the behavior of American society reveals that it's
half judaized, and the other half negrified. How can one
expect a state like that to hold together?"
> —ADOLF HITLER

"The Negro brain froze in a cold climate, inducing insan-
ity, and therefore out of kindness to the Negro, he should
be kept in the South."
> —DR. S. A. CARTWRIGHT, antebellum defender of slavery

"I confess, if I were a missionary, I would prefer to try my
hand in a country like China that has a history of two or
three or four or five thousand years, than to go into Africa
that hasn't any history at all except that which we trace to
the apes."
> —WILLIAM HOWARD TAFT, address to the Methodist Mis-
> sion Society, 1909

"By its rounded apex and less developed posterior lobe the
Negro brain resembles that of our children. . . . The
grown-up Negro partakes, as regards his intellectual facul-
ties, of the nature of the child, the female, and the senile
white. . . ."
> —CARL VOGT, celebrated German anatomist, 1864

"I don't believe in black majority rule in Rhodesia . . . not
in a thousand years."
> —IAN SMITH, prime minister of Rhodesia, 1976

"Another improvement that we made . . . was that we built our gas-chambers to accommodate two thousand people at one time."

—RUDOLF HOESS, commandant of Auschwitz

"In our striving to create better races we do not shrink from radical innovations."

—DR. WALTER GROSS, head of the Nazi Office for Racial Policy

"He who tortures animals wounds the feelings of the German people."

—HERMANN GÖRING, a sign in his Berlin office

"They undoubtedly have had a difficult Jewish problem, but why is it necessary to handle it so unreasonably?"

—CHARLES LINDBERGH, of Nazi Germany, 1938

"I don't believe for one minute that any 6,000,000 Jews were exterminated by Hitler. It never happened. The photographs you've seen passed off as pictures of dead Jews are frauds, pure and simple."

—GEORGE LINCOLN ROCKWELL, Fuehrer of the American Nazi Party, 1966

"An historic lie . . . the most tragic imposture of all time."

—ARTHUR BUTZ, in his book *The Hoax of the Twentieth Century* (1977), in which he argues that the Holocaust never took place

"[Nazi veterans are] a persecuted community."

—GENERAL SEPP DIETRICH, division commander of the Elite Guard and a former Hitler favorite, at the annual reunion of the Former Members of the Waffen S.S., 1965

"The only good Indians I ever saw were dead."

—GENERAL PHILIP SHERIDAN, 1869

"I don't go so far as to think that the only good Indians are dead Indians, but I believe nine out of every ten are, and I shouldn't inquire too closely into the case of the tenth. The most vicious cowboy has more moral principle than the average Indian."

—THEODORE ROOSEVELT

"The policy of the general government toward the red man is not only liberal, but generous."

—ANDREW JACKSON, after approving a brutal policy to remove all Indians to lands west of the Mississippi, 1830

"I don't feel we did wrong in taking this great country away from them. There were great numbers of people who needed new land, and the Indians were selfishly trying to keep it for themselves."

—JOHN WAYNE

"Just another Mexican with an opinion."

—Governor BILL CLEMENTS of Texas, referring to Dr. Jorge Bustamante, Mexico's leading immigration expert on the number and effect of illegal Mexican aliens in Texas

"Science is what one Jew copies from another."

—KARL LUEGER, mayor of Vienna in the early 1900s and a primary influence on Hitler

"Jonas Salk, Yiddish inventor of a so-called polio vaccine [is part of a Jewish plot to] mass poison American children."

—EUSTACE MULLINS, in *Women's Voice,* a hate sheet, 1955

"Life Line is not anti-Semitic, but inasmuch as there will be practically no Jews who fail to fight for Life Line, Life Line is not due to carry the torch for them."

—H. L. HUNT, explaining why his organization, Life Line, was not really anti-Semitic as had been alleged, 1964

"Christ cannot possibly have been a Jew. I don't have to prove that scientifically. It is a fact!"

—JOSEPH GOEBBELS

"The action of President [Theodore] Roosevelt in entertaining that Negro Booker T. Washington will necessitate our killing a thousand Negroes in the South before they learn their place again."

—Senator BENJAMIN R. TILLMAN of South Carolina, after
Booker T. Washington dined at the White House, 1901

"Hey, I don't mean anything by these racial cracks. There are bad Christians around too, right? It's just that, you know, a bad Jew is worse, right? You won't find any pictures of me with a swastika and a German army helmet. [As for] the blacks, most of them aren't black anyway. They're brown. Well, aren't they? It's seldom you see a really *black* black. The blacks can tell who pays lip service and who's sincere. The blacks love me."

—TED TURNER

"There is no anti-Semitism in Russia. In fact, many of my best friends are Jews."

—ALEXEI KOSYGIN, 1971

"I think they're irrelevant. . . . I think the public can understand these things. . . . I'm Jewish, and I can understand them. . . . I feel that they indicate a kind of state of mind that I feel seriously against. But nonetheless, in the running conversation of a man in high office, with a lot of things on his mind, and sometimes expressing a passionate feeling if someone's annoying him—it's not admissible—but I think it will be understood."

—Senator JACOB JAVITS, excusing the alleged anti-Semitic
remarks in Nixon's presidential tapes

"Rock 'n' roll is a means of pulling down the white man to the level of the Negro. It is part of a plot to undermine the morals of the youth of our nation."

> —The secretary of the North Alabama White Citizens' Council, May 1956

"Go to school in your own neighborhood no matter who lives there."

> —JIMMY HOFFA, on busing

"The responsibility for discrimination is not all one-sided. The Negroes, too, must share the responsibility."

> —BILLY GRAHAM, 1956

"Segregation is perfectly natural in nature. It is natural in the animal world. We do not see horses out in the meadowland lining up with cows. No; the cows go by themselves this way, and the horses by themselves the other way. Hogs and sheep keep apart. Hogs go by themselves and sheep by themselves. That general law also applies to the human race."

> —Senator THEODORE G. BILBO, in Senate debates on the Federal Employment Practices Commission, 1946

"I notice, when I go to New York, that the colored people have congregated in Harlem. That is due to an inborn instinct."

> —Senator OLIN JOHNSTON, 1946

"Your pigmentation would make you more allergic to frostbite in our frozen food."

> —An employer in Great Britain, giving a reason for not hiring a black worker

"Because their arms are too short."

> —An official of the New York Telephone Company, on why Jewish girls could not be hired to operate phone equipment, 1939

"We must ignore the tears of sobbing sentimentalists and internationalists, and we must permanently close, lock and bar the gates of our country to new immigration waves and then throw the keys away."

> —Congressman MARTIN DIES, arguing against revisions in the Immigration Act that would aid the admission of Jews escaping from Nazi Germany, 1934

"As a general policy for this country it is not good practice for us to establish a precedent . . . whereby we pass legislation which singles out groups of people by their religion or their color or their faith, or their political affiliations, either for special consideration or special penalty."

> —Congressman KARL E. MUNDT, opposing the creation of a special rescue commission for European Jewry, 1944

"The Asiatic cannot go on with our population and make a homogeneous element. The idea of comparing European immigration with an immigration that has no regard to family, that does not recognize the relation of husband and wife, that does not have the slightest degree of the ennobling and civilizing influence of the hearth stove and the fireside!"

> —Senator JAMES G. BLAINE of Maine, supporting restrictive legislation against the Chinese, 1879

"America must be kept American."

> —CALVIN COOLIDGE, signing the Immigration Restriction Act of 1924

"Those boys [Andrew Goodman and Michael Schwerner] were just artifacts, man. They weren't real. If they went to Mississippi to assuage their leaking consciences that's their business. I won't mourn for them. I have my own dead to mourn for."

> —LEROI JONES, 1965, on the two white civil rights workers killed in Mississippi

"He is a white man and so am I. Naturally I want the white man to win."

> —JACK LONDON, on the eve of Tommy Burns's defense of his world heavyweight championship against black boxer Jack Johnson (1908)

"More white people were fatally shot by police officers last year than black people [in Los Angeles]. So we don't discriminate."

> —ED DAVIS, chief of the Los Angeles Police Department, 1975

"These pigs treat us like animals."

> —LEROI JONES, referring to the Newark police, March 1976

"Violence is necessary; it is as American as cherry pie."

> —H. RAP BROWN, 1967

"All BLACK WOMEN who read this, who have birth control pills in their possession—give them back to the devil. Tell him to give them to his own women. Tell him to perform abortion and butcher up his own women. Be aware of his trick to remove your organs under pretense that they are diseased beyond repair."

> —*Muhammed Speaks,* Black Muslim newspaper, March 23, 1973

"We do not believe in violence."

> —ROBERT SHELTON, Imperial Wizard of the Ku Klux Klan, 1965. From 1954 to 1965, the Justice Department and several local police forces blamed the Klan for thirty-two bombings in Alabama, thirty-four bombings in Georgia, ten racial killings in Alabama, thirty bombings of black churches in Mississippi, the ambush killing of Colonel Lemuel Penn, the castration of an elderly black in Birmingham, and the murders of the Reverend James Reeb and Mrs. Viola Liuzzo in Alabama.

"The biggest liar in the United States."
> —J. EDGAR HOOVER on the Reverend Martin Luther King, Jr., 1966

"We have the happiest Africans in the world."
> —IAN SMITH, prime minister of Rhodesia, 1971

"Summing up, the Negro as a social group has produced but one man who would be placed among the first 15,000 or 20,000 Great Ones of Earth as judged by the usual standards— This is Alexandre Dumas. . . ."
> —EDWARD EAST, professor of genetics at Harvard, 1927

"I don't hate niggers, man. I don't—I don't—I don't associate with niggers. But on the other hand, I don't associate with common white trash or Jews or Catholics if I can help it."
> —Grand Dragon J. ROBERT JONES of North Carolina's realm of the United Klans

Robert Shelton: "The Jew or Catholic might be welcomed in the Klan if he qualified."

Playboy interviewer: "What would he have to do to qualify?"

Robert Shelton: "Give up his religion."
> —Interview with Klan Imperial Wizard ROBERT SHELTON, *Playboy*, August 1965

"There is, most unfortunately, a rapidly growing anti-Semitic feeling in the country. . . . The question for those of us who deplore such a state of things is how it can be combated and especially for those of us who are connected with colleges, how it can be combated there. . . . If every college in the country would take a limited proportion of Jews, I suspect we should go a long way toward eliminating race feeling among the students. . . . Would not the

Jews be willing to help in finding the steps best adapted for preventing the growth of race feeling among our students, and hence in the world?"

> —A. LAWRENCE LOWELL, president of Harvard University, on why, for the Jews' own good, a quota system was being introduced, 1922

"If making one million innocent Japanese uncomfortable would prevent one scheming Japanese from costing the life of one American boy, then let the million innocents suffer."

> —HENRY McLEMORE, Hearst columnist, arguing for the wartime internment of Japanese Americans, in a column called "Why Treat the Japs Well Here?," 1942

"I know I have hurt millions of persons, but I have had to do it in order to create national unity."

> —ADOLF HITLER, 1936

"Even he longs for peace, for happiness, and the chance to enjoy life."

> —JOSEPH GOEBBELS, to his diary, on Adolf Hitler, 1940

"He was a kind and polite man. That is why I can't believe Hitler wanted the war. He was the best boss I ever had."

> —GERDA CHRISTIAN, Hitler's secretary from 1933 to 1945

"What this country needs is a Hitler."

> —GENERAL NGUYEN CAO KY, when prime minister of South Vietnam

"The greatest white man."

> —STOKELY CARMICHAEL, on Adolf Hitler, 1970

"Thank God, I've always avoided persecuting my enemies."

> —ADOLF HITLER, 1941

WOULD YOU MIND SAYING THAT AGAIN, PLEASE?

"Telling it like it is means telling it like it was and how it is now that it isn't what it was to the now people."
—JILL JOHNSTON, *The Village Voice*, 1968

"I would be batting the big feller if they wasn't ready with the other one, but a left-hander would be the thing if they wouldn't have knowed it already because there is more things involved than could come up on the road, even after we've been home for a long while."
—CASEY STENGEL

"Given a syntactically ambiguous grammar, it is possible to use semantic information to disambiguate its syntax and construct a similar unambiguous grammar."
—H. WILLIAM BUTTLEMANN, in his Ph.D. thesis, *Syntax-Semantics Systems as Structure Manipulation Systems: Phrase Structure Grammars and Generalized Finite Automata*

"Because the self is of unmanifested nature, and because man's life is always in the field of the manifested, it is not to be wondered at if some people hear about it with great surprise, and others are not able to understand it at all."
—MAHARISHI MAHESH YOGI

"It doesn't mean if you don't believe in nothing that it's nothing. You have to treat the nothing as if it were something."
—ANDY WARHOL

"This is the core-happening here. We're trying to get our heads together, our whole being together, intellectually, emotionally, socially, sexually, all the component parts of our beings into ... self-actualizing persons. ... From there, we want to go ahead and maximize our potential for community."
—An instructor at Sandstone, an experimental "love community" outside Los Angeles where 275 member couples experimented with open sex, early 1970s

"Remember, we are not representing Heaven as a place geographically, but a state of consciousness, wherein all men can arise to, and recognize, God's Presence as Real, as tangibleatable, and as practical as the principles of mathematics; it is indeed wonderful. Not only tangibleated but as tangibleatable; it can and will continue to materialize, and repersonify, rematerialize, and repersonify, for the great materializing process is going on."
—FATHER DIVINE (George Baker)

"Consciousness - energy - love - awareness - light - wisdom - beauty-truth-purity. It's all the SAME. Any trip you want to take leads to the SAME place."
—BABA RAM DASS

"I believe one can know the unknowable, but only in perfect silence. We realize the utter futility of trying to speak the unspeakable. But there is a delightful pointlessness and mystery about it all that makes life so beautiful."
— JOHN MCLAUGHLIN, jazz-rock guitarist, 1976

"Yes, I listen to the trees and hear what *they* say and I think that they hear what I say. Not what I *say*, since trees don't speak English, but the trees are very aware of what I'm doing to them. . . . And by me I don't mean Timothy Leary. They don't talk that language."
— TIMOTHY LEARY, *The Politics of Ecstasy* (1968)

"The oldest traditions place the fundamental trait of our existence into this singular kind of bifurcation. It [gender] constitutes an ambiguous complementarity, different from both a mirror image and a shadow. As duality, it is distinct from the positive copy of a negative and from the deterministic match of DNA's double helix. I assume it to be the foundation of metaphor and poetic speech—the only appropriate mode to express it."
— IVAN ILLICH, *Gender* (1983)

"God speaks to you physically on a metabolic level, and the universe runs the shit to you and tells you what's righteous and what isn't."
— ROB TYNER, rock performer

"Nothing can be attained without suffering, but at the same time one must begin by sacrificing suffering."
— GEORGES IVANOVITCH GURDJIEFF (1877–1949)

"But, gentlemen, I maintain we should turn a deaf ear to any other red herring that may be drawn across our path."
— Report of a speech in *All Too True* (1954), by Denys Parsons

"She's experiencing a traumatic sense of personal expansion but in the sensational, egotistical way characteristic of the vulgar side of Hearst greatness."

> —PATRICK TOBIN, Patty Hearst's tour guide on a trip to Europe and her cultural mentor, explaining her behavior during captivity

"There is a mutual causal relationship between patterns of action and structures of meaning, so that over time the meanings of persons join together to produce patterns of action, and those patterns of actions are used to reconstruct persons' meanings, so that you have a coevolution of structures of meaning and patterns of action."

> —VERNON E. CRONEN, professor of communications studies at the University of Massachusetts, on his theory of communication, 1982

"Nothing means nothing, but it isn't really nothing because nothing is something that it isn't."

> —DARRYL DAWKINS, center for the Philadelphia 76ers basketball team, just before he took a vow of silence with sportswriters, 1978

BETTER LEFT
UNSAID

"Fat people pollute the esthetic environment."
> —Attributed to Cloris Leachman in *People* magazine, May 3, 1976. She denies having made the remark, which aroused considerable ire.

"If I were an American boy ... I'd rather not have a French and a British soldier beside me, one on my right and one on my left."
> —Secretary of State JOHN FOSTER DULLES, in answer to a query from Senator Wayne Morse on why our French and English allies were not working in tandem with U.S. troops in the Mideast, 1957

"The most famous stablemates since Joseph and Mary."
> —DICK SCHAAP, sportscaster, of champion race horses Riva Ridge and Secretariat, 1974. He later apologized.

"We're more popular than Jesus now."
> —JOHN LENNON, on the Beatles' fame, 1966

"I see nothing wrong with ethnic purity being maintained."
> —JIMMY CARTER as a presidential candidate, 1976

"Have you ever lived in the suburbs? I haven't, but I've talked to people who have, and it's sterile. It's nothing; it's wasting your life."
> —New York mayor ED KOCH, interview in *Playboy*, April 1982

"The Karen Ann Quinlan of American cities."
> —SHIRLEY MACLAINE, on New York City, said onstage at the Palace Theater, 1976

THE TRUTH

"In the midst of all dwells the sun, and so, as if seated upon a royal throne, the sun rules the family of planets as they circle around him."
—NICOLAUS COPERNICUS (1473–1543)

"There is one thing about being President, nobody can tell you when to sit down."
—Attributed to DWIGHT D. EISENHOWER

"You cannot conquer America!"
—WILLIAM PITT, THE ELDER, in a speech to Parliament, 1777

"How often the deepest convictions of one generation are the rejects of the next."
—Judge LEARNED HAND

"Be cheerful while you are alive."
—Ptahhotep, 27th century B.C.

"Keep breathing."

> —SOPHIE TUCKER, when asked the secret of longevity on her eightieth birthday, January 13, 1964

"One of the countless drawbacks of being in Congress is that I am compelled to receive impertinent letters from a jackass like you in which you say I promised to have the Sierra Madre mountains reforested and I have been in Congress two months and haven't done it. Will you please take two running jumps and go to hell."

> —Congressman JOHN STEVEN MCGROARTY of California, to a constituent, 1934

"There is no such thing as inevitable war. If war comes it will be from failure of human wisdom."

> —BONAR LAW (1858–1923)

"Eureka! I have found it!"

> —Archimedes (c. 287–212 B.C.), upon discovering the principle of buoyancy while in the bathtub

"$E = mc^2$" (Energy equals mass times the speed of light squared.)

> —ALBERT EINSTEIN

"If we hadn't used oil as a political weapon, today nobody would listen to us."

> —SHEIKH AHMAD ZAKI YAMANI

"I don't believe in this mandate stuff. A guy runs for office and gets elected. All of a sudden he's got a mandate. Two less votes and he's nothing."

> —GEORGE MEANY, head of the AFL–CIO, on the November 1974 elections

"There are times when a cigar is only a cigar."

> —SIGMUND FREUD

INDEX